WORSHIP
THAT WORKS

WORSHIP THAT WORKS

Theory and Practice
for Unitarian Universalists

Wayne Arnason
and
Kathleen Rolenz

SKINNER HOUSE BOOKS
BOSTON

Copyright © 2008 by Wayne B. Arnason and Kathleen C. Rolenz. All rights reserved. Published by Skinner House Books, an imprint of the Unitarian Universalist Association of Congregations, a liberal religious organization with more than 1,000 congregations in the U.S. and Canada, 25 Beacon St., Boston, MA 02108-2800.

Printed in the United States.

Text and cover design by Bruce Jones

ISBN 1-55896-526-2
978-1-55896-526-3

5 4 3 2 1
10 09 08 07

Library of Congress Cataloging-in-Publication Data

Arnason, Wayne B. (Wayne Bergthor), 1950-
   Worship that works : theory and practice for Unitarian Universalists / Wayne B. Arnason and Kathleen C. Rolenz.
       p. cm.
   ISBN-13: 978-1-55896-526-3 (pbk. : alk. paper)
   ISBN-10: 1-55896-526-2 (pbk. : alk. paper) 1. Unitarian Universalist Association. 2. Worship. I. Rolenz, Kathleen. II. Title.

BX9853.A43 2007
264'.09132--dc22
                                                           2007011921

This book is dedicated to the members and staff of West Shore Unitarian Universalist Church in Rocky River, Ohio, with whom we share our weekly worship life. Their encouragement and support made our sabbatical dream of traveling the country in search of transformative worship come true.

CONTENTS

INTRODUCTION

It was a bleak January Sunday in Cleveland, and neither one of us felt like going to church. Normally, when one of us feels this way, the other has the energy to help us both rise to the occasion. It's one of the great blessings of being co-ministers who are married to each other. On this particular day, however, we both felt like the guy in the old joke, who wakes up one Sunday and immediately starts complaining to his spouse.

"I hate the service! The hymns are boring, the readings are pedantic, the sermons are obscure, and after it's over, I get the feeling that nobody there likes me. I'm not going to church this Sunday!"

"Sweetheart," his long-suffering spouse gently replies, "the people in the congregation don't hate you and the service isn't all that bad, but besides that, you've got to go. You're the minister!"

We were able to climb out of our valley of the shadow that particular Sunday and do a workmanlike job on the service we had planned. Indeed, we found it easy to remember that our congregation did like us, and the service was pretty good after all. Beyond that morning, however, we were becoming aware of a deeper dissatisfaction with our role as worship leaders and with the state of Unitarian Universalist worship as a whole. We knew we hadn't always felt this way.

Our personal involvement in the study of worship has its roots in our personal histories and our spiritual practices. For Wayne, a born and bred UU, worship as the center of spiritual practice has been a passion that began in 1977 with his involvement in the Unitarian Universalist liturgical order known as the Congregation of Abraxas. Wayne's interest in an ordered life of worship and practice has continued in recent years through a Zen Buddhist discipline to which he has been committed since 1995. Kathleen came to Unitarian Universalist ministry from a Christian background that she had rejected, and then struggled with again during her years as a UU student in a United Methodist seminary. She has rediscovered her Christian identity through scriptural studies and pastoral ministry and found it affirmed through her involvement in the worship life of the UU Christian Fellowship.

So we are a married couple sharing a Unitarian Universalist co-ministry, leading worship at West Shore UU Church near Cleveland, engaging personally in well-defined traditions of spiritual practice from world religious traditions, and finding opportunities to engage in the worship forms that surround those practices. As a Christian Unitarian Universalist, Kathleen seeks out occasional participation in Christian worship and has been active in creating interfaith worship opportunities with clergy from other traditions. As a UU who practices Buddhism, Wayne participates regularly in Zen liturgies.

Despite our roles as worship leaders and our involvement in the worship life of other churches and traditions, we were growing steadily dissatisfied with how much we knew about the trees and how little about the forest of worship at the beginning of the twenty-first century. Most of the time, we were engaged from Sunday to Sunday with the details of designing and leading services at West Shore. We had a distant understanding that worship was a hot topic in the mainline Protestant world. A revolution in Protestant worship had already taken place right under our noses in the large evangelical congregations described as "megachurches"—so named because they attract at least 2,000 people in a typical weekly service. Younger generations of Protestant evangelicals who grew up in these churches were now beginning to explore older and more intimate worship forms in a movement known as the "emergent church." This style of worship seeks to engage parishioners in a direct, unmediated experience of God. There were websites and blogs and conferences about this phenomenon, but we didn't know much about it. In fact, neither of us had attended very many Christian worship services outside of our liberal Protestant bubble in recent years. We also found that we had only rare opportunities to attend services led by our UU colleagues because we were usually committed to the worship life of our own congregation.

Our dissatisfaction didn't affect our passion for worship or worship leadership. In seven years of service at West Shore, we started a well-received worship associates program and developed a cadre of experienced and trained lay leaders. We experimented with the worship format and offered well-attended classes and conferences on worship arts. We encouraged the congregation to abandon a poorly attended first service in our large sanctuary and replaced it with formats for alternative worship in the social hall. We felt we had learned a lot together about worship that "works" to create growth and depth in the life of the congregation. We needed no convincing about the fact that worship that *changes lives*, what we call "transformative worship," is a critical component in the health of a Unitarian Universalist congregation.

Still, our efforts to add alternative services at West Shore left us feeling like something was missing. Deep down, we wanted our worship leadership and participation to encourage and reflect the powerful transformation that the liberal church had brought about in our own lives. Watching nationally broadcast evangelical services, we recognized that they were rarely about the fine points of Christian doctrine, but they did directly address and illustrate lives changing for the better because of church involvement. We had to admit to ourselves that too often our own worship services and those we had experienced in other UU congregations lacked this transformational dimension. We each felt that our approach to leading worship in our own congregation was becoming stagnant.

The light at the end of this tunnel of dissatisfaction was a sabbatical leave that began in the fall of 2005. It offered a unique opportunity to engage anew with the diversity and creativity of worship forms within our own tradition and those of other faiths. We decided to drive all over the country visiting churches and colleagues we'd always wanted to visit, both UU and non-UU, and to write a blog about our experiences. We knew we were looking for worship that would be transformative for *us*, that "worked" for us by moving and engaging us, and that would change our lives for the better.

During the fall of 2004, we took exploratory presabbatical trips whenever we had opportunities to travel. The first visit we wrote about was to the mother of all megachurches: Willow Creek Community Church, in the western suburbs of Chicago. We visited Willow Creek on the weekend after Thanksgiving in 2004. The final congregation we visited, as the sabbatical ended in December 2005, was Saddleback Community Church, founded by best-selling author Rick Warren, whose books *The Purpose-Driven Church* and *The Purpose-Driven Life* have greatly influenced both church life and popular culture. In between these two megachurch bookends, we attended services or interviewed worship leaders at thirty congregations of diverse sizes and traditions, about equally divided between Unitarian Universalism and other faiths. We also reviewed and studied the current literature about Protestant worship, including recent trends.

Initially, we were drawn to this kind of a sabbatical by our well-established commitment to worship as a spiritual practice. As we traveled, we discovered and rediscovered elements and experiences of worship that were deeply important to each of us personally. Yet, we also discovered something about our Unitarian Universalism movement as a whole: There is a gap between what our congregations offer in worship and what is rapidly becoming standard in the larger Protestant culture. We worry about what this gap will mean for us as the twenty-first century unfolds. Worship is not the only engine that drives the health of a church, but without compelling worship that moves people towards lives of wholeness, service, and joy, a church community is at best self-sustaining and ingrown, and at worst a slowly dying artifact of a passing era.

We came away from our sabbatical convinced that a renewal of engagement with worship in congregations of all sizes is critical if

Unitarian Universalism is to survive and thrive in the twenty-first century. Lacking strong traditions of spiritual practice and outflanked in our ability to engage with innovative worship possibilities, Unitarian Universalism could be on the edge of a decline into irrelevance.

We could also be poised to renew and revitalize our congregational worship life. Our worries have been balanced by many signs of hope. In 2002, the president of the Unitarian Universalist Association, William Sinkford, called for an association-wide conversation about how we use the language of reverence. That same year "Liturgy and Ritual" was taken up as a theme by the Prairie Group, a bellwether study group of UU clergy devoted to quality scholarship and honest debate. Many midsized and large congregations have been experiencing exciting innovations in their worship life under the leadership of a new generation of UU clergy. In 2004, the UUA General Assembly in Long Beach initiated a "seeker service" (designed for newcomers) on Sunday mornings, using rock music, drama, projection screens, and original songs and hymns. This was to reach out to an unchurched community that might be attracted by media coverage of our General Assembly. The 2005 General Assembly worship was enlivened by the leadership of younger music directors and the introduction of the first hymnal supplement since the publication of *Singing the Living Tradition* in 1995. *Singing the Journey* introduced seventy-four new songs from a variety of cultures, traditions, and styles of music. The team that compiled the supplement offered thoughtful reflections on issues in contemporary UU worship in web-published essays and introductory workshops. Seminary classes, districts, and UUMA chapters have taken up the study of our worship traditions and the growing edges of our worship life. In 2007, the UUA's Office of Young Adult and Campus Ministries sponsored the first national UU conference on Contemporary Worship. Unitarian Universalists want to create and experience worship that works.

We wrote this book for a Unitarian Universalist audience, recognizing that those in other free-church traditions might also find it useful. The challenges of worship in the Unitarian Universalist tradition, however, are unique. Despite the broad tent that our friends in such denominations as the United Church of Christ, the Disciples of Christ, and the United Methodists must now support to shelter their internal diversity, they continue to be unequivocally Christian, with a worship lineage that they trace to the beginnings of their traditions. Unitarians and Universalists abandoned an exclusively Christian identity in the early part of the twentieth century, but our worship life (outside of a few congregations) was slow to reflect that important decision. There has been very little published by Unitarian Universalists that has offered a comprehensive theory of Unitarian Universalist worship or described the diversity of its best practices. The two current extremes of our worship practice are, at one end, idiosyncratic services that reflect only the religious ideology and creativity of the worship leader, and at the other, services that are firmly embedded in only one of our theological identities. In the middle, we find most of our congregations offering worship that at best creatively engages our theological diversity and at worst speaks to the lowest common denominator theology within a particular congregation.

Worship is a hot topic these days, and it should be. It is time for Unitarian Universalists to regain the place we once held on the cutting edge of congregational worship. It is time to ask ourselves what transformative worship means in our lives, and how we will create it for upcoming generations. We hope that this book will be of interest to those who create worship for their congregations and those with a broader interest in worship theory, history, and innovation among Unitarian Universalists. We also hope it will speak to issues in worship planning for congregations of different sizes; and that what it reveals about Unitarian Universalist worship will be useful to readers for years to come.

VISIONS AND CHALLENGES

On the last day of our sabbatical, we watched a beautiful winter sunset from the balcony surrounding the education building at Saddleback Community Church in Southern California. We were at the church that probably best represented the gap between our UU worship practices and those of the liberal and evangelical Protestant congregations now attracting new members of diverse generations and cultures at a much faster pace than our congregations. Saddleback has as many as fifteen different worship experiences to choose from over the course of every three-day weekend of services. We had just attended their anchor service in the sanctuary, a worship experience using the order of service that has redefined evangelical worship: power-pop praise songs, a simple liturgy focusing on prayer, and a long sermon with memorable hooks and visual aids. Despite the high energy and strong congregational response, we found it boring.

We wondered whether that was the source of the gap we had been noticing between UU and contemporary Protestant worship. Perhaps people attracted to Unitarian Universalism are a different breed from those who attend these huge evangelical churches. Perhaps we are so smart, sophisticated, and self-assured that we don't fall for the worship style these churches seem to use so successfully.

We decided that before we left the Saddleback campus we would check out one of the other services being offered that evening, the Ohana service, which featured hula. It grabbed our attention when we first read the signboard listing the worship choices. A little cynical and somewhat jaded, we headed over to the tent that would soon host the service; maybe there would be someone setting up who could tell us what hula worship was all about.

We found a lovely Hawaiian woman who was more than happy to tell us why Saddleback had the Ohana service. There were Hawaiian members of Saddleback Church who felt that their lives had been transformed by their encounter with the congregation and its message. A significant population of Hawaiians in the region might be attracted to a service that reflects the sacred musical and dance traditions of their culture. The Hawaiian members did not want to miss the message that was heard in the main sanctuary, but they wanted the intimacy of a worshiping community that reflected their heritage. So they offer a videocast of the same sermon heard in the main worship hall that day, framed by the music and cultural traditions of Hawaii.

A driving force behind the growth explosion in conservative churches over the past thirty years has been the small-group ministry movement, through which large churches re-create the intimate atmosphere of small congregations. Most successful large and growing congregations in North America have followed the same formula with their worship offerings, and the Ohana service was one example. Members of Saddleback, with a congregation of more than fifteen thousand, could choose from the same-sized weekly worship services, classes, and small-group experiences available to a congregation of three hundred people, all of whom come from the same cultural niche.

Saddleback had separate services for those who liked their worship loud, for those who liked more singing than sermon, for singles, for younger adults, for people who wanted passionate praise in a service, for Spanish speakers, for Hawaiian Islanders, and yes, for those who preferred traditional worship and hymns. What these congregants all had in common is that they had found the worship life and message of the church transformational in their lives.

We thought about what our congregation would look like if our model for worship incorporated some of the best designs we had encountered in our travels. Our newsletter might say:

This Sunday at West Shore Church the worship team led by Revs. Kathleen Rolenz and Wayne Arnason will lead three services, at 9:00 AM, 11:00 AM, and 11:11 AM. The 9 AM service in Baker Hall is intergenerational and features the Free Spirit Band, worship stations, and an interactive sermon on this month's theme. It will be followed by church school for all ages, and our morning forum and breakfast during the ten o'clock hour.

The eleven o'clock traditional service is in the sanctuary and features our organist, classical musicians, and choir, with longer periods of silent meditation and prayer and a sermon on this month's theme informed by the modern and ancient scriptures of humanity. The 11:11 service features the Free Spirit Band, leading our Creation Spirituality service in the round in Baker Hall. Our second session of church school is available during the eleven o'clock hour.

Worship opportunities during the week include our weekly Wednesday evening Vespers featuring Taize chant, our monthly first Thursday UU Christian Fellowship service with communion, our second Saturday night Earth Spirit service, and our weekly Buddhist sitting group on Tuesdays, with a preceding full Soto chant service on the last Tuesday of each month.

This is an achievable vision for us, based in the cultural communities and worship preferences already present in our particular congregation, but as of 2007, we are not there yet. It's a vision that a few Unitarian Universalist congregations are on their way to realizing, in their own distinct way. If we could develop a worship life this rich and diverse, it would simply mean that we were catching up with the twenty-first-century style and variety of worship offerings already available in hundreds of vital mainline Protestant and evangelical congregations of diverse sizes.

Nothing New Under the Sun

It was a sunny Sunday morning, the first we would experience on our sabbatical journey. We had just emerged from the subway on New York City's Upper West Side, and we were searching for one of the cathedrals of American Protestantism, The Riverside Church. Down a side street, we spotted the spire of a massive Gothic structure that stood out against the glass and chrome of nearby buildings. We entered the narthex and found our way to the sanctuary just in time for the grand processional to begin.

The Riverside Church is one of the most renowned pulpits in America. The church was built between 1926 and 1930 during the ministry of Harry Emerson Fosdick. More recently, William Sloane Coffin and James Forbes served the church. The service offered us some of the best quality Protestant worship we'd ever experienced. It was not particularly innovative: no big screens, no PowerPoint presentations, no pop-rock songs. The color and pageantry in the service was provided by the banners in the processional representing the church's ministries, the choir's beautiful robes and voices, the magnificent organ, and the vivid illustrations within the sermon. In its embrace of the great traditions of Protestant liturgy, done with excellence and grandeur, the service at Riverside was unsurpassable. We came away knowing we had been to church.

"There is nothing new under the sun," laments the poet in Ecclesiastes. When it comes to worship, there are many who would say, "That's fine with me!" Indeed, there may be no field of study where this lament seems more appropriate. Rooted in profound human experiences of awe, wonder, fear, and family, the impulse to worship is an original response to finding ourselves alive. Worship as devotion, as storytelling, as metaphorical ritual, and as a response to the mystery of life has played its role in human communities through rites, liturgical forms, and traditions. Almost by definition, the first thing most participants in worship come searching for is the ancient, the familiar, the experience outside of time.

We also come in search of transformation: from daily experience to transcendent experience; from our ordinary seeing to extraordinary vision; from our routine life to unpredictable meanings.

The tensions between the desires for the familiar and the transformative require that our worship be open to change. It can be argued that in North American Catholic and Protestant worship there has been more widespread and accelerated innovation during the last half of the twentieth century than in any century since the Protestant Reformation. Two of the most obvious worship innovations include the Vatican II (1962 – 1965) decision to offer Catholic Mass in the vernacular and the widespread adoption of technologically sophisticated seeker services during the 1980s and 1990s by evangelical congregations. Now the emergent church movement is offering fresh creativity, transforming evangelical worship. Christian worship, which had seen very little new under the sun for generations, is suddenly open to many new possibilities.

These possibilities, however, have had little impact in the free congregations that inherited the Radical Reformation traditions of worship. Among the liberal religions, Unitarian Universalism has come away curiously untouched by this revolution, despite the absence of a central authority.

There is certainly a story to be told of twentieth-century creativity in worship within Unitarian Universalism. The time period began with older Protestant Christian worship forms dominant in our congregations. The decision to be radically noncreedal opened up possibilities for worship life that our ancestors could not have imagined: scripture texts from non-Christian religions; a communion ritual based on flowers or water; hymnody rooted in a humanist theology; earth-centered rituals inserted into a Protestant order of service. Although these innovations became an accepted part of Unitarian Universalist tradition, the overall form of worship in most of our congregations did not change much. The seventeenth-century Puritan Protestant order of worship still dominates our congregations, even those that have stripped away the Christian and theistic sources behind these forms.

Is that a problem? This style of worship is rooted in our culture. At its best, it has all the elements of timeless familiarity that most people want, with enough room for innovative forms that speak to changing values and keep the possibility of transformative power fresh. At its worst, this style of worship is highly intellectual, disembodied, and elitist, locked within a seventeenth-century European cultural ghetto.

Because this has also been true of many mainline Protestant traditions, and because Unitarian Universalism has seen modest benefits in membership from the mainline decline and the ongoing Catholic defections, we have been complacent and sometimes even militant about avoiding recent innovations in worship.

Our members and ministers often decry the hi-tech approach of the evangelicals, viewing it as one more sign of the fundamentalist climate in which we live. We flip past channels that broadcast megachurch arena preachers, and we rarely experience them firsthand. Few of us keep up with the literature of worship or with current developments in worship life in mainline Protestant or evangelical congregations that are kin to us. For clergy especially, the weekly challenge of engaging with the culture and traditions of worship in our congregations, as well as the creative process of sermon and service preparation, makes us the worship experts in our congregations. Our expertise, however, is too often the expertise of a thousand details. It is difficult to engage our congregations in owning a broad vision of why we worship.

In the 2005 report of the Commission on Appraisal of the Unitarian Universalist Association, entitled "Engaging Our Theological Diversity," the commissioners commented: "Few laypersons and equally few ministers are adequately prepared to plan worship that is inviting and acceptable to UUs of all theological stripes without reducing worship to the least common denominator in a way that leaves everyone in attendance unoffended but also unfulfilled."

When worship life becomes a focus for conflict in a congregation, it is usually about the details. What kinds of music are acceptable? Do lay-led services have to have the same form as minister-led services? Do we have responsive readings, a talk-back, or Joys and Concerns? Should we have two services, and if so, should they be the same or different? When we experience such conflicts, we are often surprised to find out how much our members really do care. We become aware that the conversation needs to shift from whether our worship should ever change to how we can best use our resources to ensure healthy change.

The Primacy of Worship

Just before we began our travels, we were standing on a street corner in downtown Cleveland waiting for a light to change when an elderly woman joined us and struck up a conversation. "Lovely afternoon, isn't it?" she said, flashing a large smile. We exchanged pleasantries, and then we realized that her presence was not merely happenstance: She had zeroed in on us to talk about her church.

"I just wanted to tell you about my church. It's the Four Square Gospel Church of East Cleveland, and I just love it and wanted to share it with you."

Her presence was so nonthreatening and so positive that we took a moment to talk with her, thinking what a good sermon illustration this might make some day.

"It's the worship," the woman whispered confidentially. "You go to worship at my church and you come out feeling like a changed person."

We accepted one of her brochures, thanked the woman, and parted company. What was it, we wondered later, that would inspire an elderly woman to wander the streets of downtown Cleveland to pass out brochures for her church? The woman herself had answered the question: It was the experience of worship that made a difference in her life. We asked ourselves: Could the same ever be true for members of our own church?

Von Ogden Vogt, one of the greatest twentieth-century Unitarian liturgists, titled one of his books *The Primacy of Worship*. We too believe that worship is primary; all other activities and purposes of congregational life emerge from its worship life. We believe this is true not only regarding the institutional realities of church life, but also regarding how a congregation interprets its identity and articulates its mission. This is because the worship experience is the most important way that a church tells the story of lives transformed by participation in the free church community, and sends its members forth to tell the world that story.

Institutionally, worship is primary because without some form of regular worship service, there is no church community. You can have focus groups that talk about how to be a church. You can have lectures that offer new knowledge or prophetic engagement with the issues of the day. You can have religious education classes to teach the doctrines and values of your tradition. You can have social events and fund-raisers and parties that build community. You can have service projects and social justice demonstrations that engage people in living out their liberal religious beliefs. However, until you open the doors for public worship, no one in the world, inside our tradition or outside it, is going to identify you as a church.

During one stop on our sabbatical, we experienced worship planning that told the story of how the church community is changing lives. We visited and interviewed Rev. Ken Beldon, founding pastor of a new UU church in the Philadelphia suburbs. At this point, the church had just three things: a name (Wellsprings), an office, and a minister. As Ken described the care they were taking in creating the founding culture of the congregation, we immediately realized that he was familiar with the metaphor of congregational DNA. Church growth consultants have used the metaphor of DNA (the genetic code embodied in all our human cells) to convey the idea that a new congregation's mission, values, and culture must be intentionally established before it begins public worship. (See "Qualities of Transformative Worship.") Through small focus groups, the Wellsprings organizers were naming and holding up the life-transforming experiences of Unitarian Universalist community and practice that the experienced members had already undergone. They were also identifying the hungers and needs for transformation expressed by people newly attracted to these focus groups by the liberal religious message.

The plan for birthing the Wellsprings congregation involved

a two-year startup process, with public worship not scheduled to open until the last half of their second year. The founding leadership of the congregation realized that holding public worship services crossed a threshold of recognition by the surrounding community as a functioning church. They did not want to cross that threshold until they were well along in creating a culture of religious community that was already making a difference in people's lives. Wellsprings began their public worship services using a contemporary format on schedule early in 2007.

The bylaws of the Unitarian Universalist Association recognize the primacy of worship, listing "holding regular religious services" as the first of only three *sine qua non* requirements a group must satisfy to demonstrate that they are indeed a congregation. (The other two are holding an annual business meeting and keeping records of membership.) Being recognized by the Association as a church was not something that Wellsprings was anxious to schedule, however. They felt that the decision to apply for UUA membership would emerge as the right decision at the right time, a time when public worship was successfully proclaiming a life-changing message that was attracting people to join the congregation's founders.

As far as the UUA bylaws are concerned, it doesn't matter where you worship or whether others might recognize the space you use as sacred. It doesn't matter what day or time you gather or whether the order of your worship has any elements rooted in Unitarian Universalist practices. Bylaws, however, are limited in what they can invoke regarding a congregation's or a denomination's identity.

We all know that it *does* matter where you worship. The key issue is not the type of building; during our travels, we attended worship services in converted Safeway stores, church basements, and elementary schools. The key issue is how the space is transformed into sacred space when it is used for worship. That change is emblematic of the transformative potential of the service that is about to happen and the tradition that it represents.

It also matters whether the worship happens at times when people can make space in their lives for it and that the culture of the local community supports as appropriate. Finally, the content matters. It matters that the worship contains elements recognizable as a Unitarian Universalist service. In the last half of the twentieth century, the use of a flaming chalice symbol, a common hymnal or body of hymns, and traditional words of covenant became the most common markers that told people they had entered a Unitarian Universalist worshipping community. The Commission on Appraisal believes that content matters, and has framed that concern in a very broad recommendation that the UUA develop new worship resources that are "theologically welcoming."

We believe that there is something further, something that matters even more than content, that is crucial to how a worshipping community understands itself. That something is the attitude a community brings to worship. What do they think they are doing when they attend worship services? Are they coming to find intellectual stimulation or to hear stories of lives that have been changed? Can you tell by the way they come into the space what entering into worship means to this congregation? Is transformative meaning conveyed by the way the worship leaders approach their roles? What does the order of service and how it is presented reveal about this congregation and its understanding of the religion?

In our interviews, we asked worship leaders with a wide range of theological orientations two initial questions: What is worship and why do people come to worship? For our Christian friends from traditions outside our own, the first answer was always some variation on "We come together to worship God." Our colleagues in the liberal church offered a variety of different responses.

Rev. Earl Holt, senior minister of the predominantly Christian King's Chapel in Boston, responded immediately: "We come together to worship the Lord! We come together to be saved." His elucidation of the meanings of "worship the Lord" and "saved" reflected his liberal Christianity. Many more of our colleagues based their first responses on the definition found in the 1982 Commission on Common Worship (CCW) essay available on the UUA Worship Web Internet site (www.uua.org/spirituallife/worshipweb). The CCW definition refers to the ancient English root of the word *worship* (*woerscippen*), which can be translated into "considering things of worth." They said that the purpose of worship was to lift up the highest and holiest of human values. This approach was the basis for many psychological and anthropological definitions of worship that we heard. Rev. Ken Belden said that "worship is a public act of reaching into ourselves— it is a transformative act of deepening and it is leading people to a place where they want to go." Rev. Laurel Hallman of First Unitarian Church in Dallas said that "worship is a communal ritual event with a covenanted community that both links to its past and allows for the elements of creative surprise." Rev. Dennis Hamilton did not see much difference between psychology and spirituality: "The minister's job is to help people be more engaged with life. We engage them with mysteries beyond words; mysteries that can only be engaged by music, metaphor and symbol." Rev. Kendyl Gibbons warned us about the perils of seeking a common definition of worship. She said, "The purpose of worship is not to talk about the ineffable; the point is whether or not you can enact it. Enacting it may not require talking about it. That's my goal: to seduce people into an experience [of worship] whether they understand what I'm doing or not."

In these diverse responses lies both the promise of liberal religious worship, and the problem. Within our tradition, we are able to say: "Worship means praising, confessing, and discerning the word of God." We are able to say: "Worship is a private transformation done in the context of corporate ceremony and ritual." We are able to say: "Worship is when we hold up things of worth and value. It is our link to the past and a gateway to our future." We are able to say: "No matter what our definition of worship might be, we have an embodied experience of being in worship together, and that is what is most important."

All of these understandings have integrity within this tradition that honors the mystery of life and recognizes that what is invisible and essential to our lives can be made visible and manifest. All these understandings are available to the worship leader and worship team.

Is it a problem that we have no common understanding of what we are actually worshiping? If there is, in fact, no transcendent reality to whom all praises should flow, then is the worship service in our tradition like a house built on the shifting sands of individual or congregational theologies?

The Presence of the Holy

On a Sunday morning in San Francisco, we were excited to discover the congregation and liturgy of St. Gregory's Episcopal Church in the Portrero Hill neighborhood. We had heard that St. Gregory's was known for its innovative liturgy, which had adapted and incorporated ancient Christian and Jewish practices. We were captivated by the "bells and smells" of their worship: the high liturgical vestments, the swinging of incense and censures, the complete attention given to involving all the senses in worship.

At one point in the service, a large, beautifully bound edition of the Bible was lifted up by the priest and paraded through the congregation, much as Jews do with the Torah. Everyone was invited to touch the Bible as it passed by or, if that was not possible, to touch the shoulder of someone who had touched the Bible. As the book wound through the throng, there was the sense of being part of a living stream of history and tradition. The action moved private and daily devotion to the Bible into a public act of worship and reverence. It was a clarifying moment, a moment when we felt especially moved to be in the presence of the holy.

At St. Gregory's, the meaning and purpose of gathering was very clear from the beginning: to worship God. In many worship traditions, the meaning and purpose is made clear in every component of the service from beginning to end. In Unitarian Universalist church settings, that clarity often depends on the size of the congregation, but our perception is that what usually happens is something like this:

Members who know each other are talking among themselves inside and outside the worship space. People with clipboards are milling around asking you to sign this petition or join in on this project, committee, or cause. Some of this activity may spill over from the foyer or social hall into the sanctuary. Children are dashing to their classrooms. Parents are hurriedly trying to detach from their children and grab a cup of coffee before the service begins. They come into the service late, hoping to avoid announcements. A prelude is playing but no one is really listening; they are busy talking. The opening words of the service—often "Good morning!"—are the signal for some to come into the sanctuary. Finally, about ten minutes into the service, the last people have entered, settled themselves into their seats, and let go of enough of their lives to be open to what is happening in the service.

Whenever we attend a service that begins like that, Kathleen can't help but think of her homiletics professor, who asked a class one day: "What's the worst thing you can do in worship?" Kathleen has written about her response to hearing that question:

> My mind was reeling. I could think of several things—forgetting my sermon, tipping over the chalice, delivering a terribly awkward prayer. The professor paused for a moment and then said, "Breaking the silence before the service with 'Good morning.'" I was astonished. I thought, That's what we do in every UU church I've ever attended. He continued: "People come together in worship to be reminded that they stand in the presence of the holy."

The presence of the holy! We wonder how many members of Unitarian Universalist churches when asked why they came to worship, would respond: "To be in the presence of the holy."

Actually, we suspect more than ever before. The word *holy* used to be one of those tricky words that you had to be prepared to defend with a precise definition before using it in a Unitarian Universalist church. Rev. Dr. William F. Schulz, the last self-identified humanist to be elected president of the Unitarian Universalist Association, turned a corner for us in a report to our 1986 General Assembly. Schulz observed: "Reason is still a cherished standard in our religious repertoire, but reason is coming to be supplemented by our immediate apprehension of the holy and by our conviction that the holy is embodied in the abundance of a scarred creation."

It wasn't a definition of the holy, but it was an acknowledgement that the universe in which humanity dwells remains fundamentally mysterious to us, despite the many advances we have made towards understanding it. The "apprehension of the holy" is an experience that exists both in time and out of time, an experience where body and mind drop away and we have a sense of beauty, awe, and oneness with the world around us. Most people report having such singular and defining experiences, or less dramatic but more frequent experiences of holy moments. They are experiences that transcend theology, for they confirm the faith of the believer and remind the nonbeliever that experiencing the holy is also part of being human.

We believe that the apprehension of the holy is an experience human beings have in common. Worship is a human activity located at the crossroads where the apprehension of the holy and the living of daily life meet. Insofar as the meaning of our lives can be transformed by the apprehension of the holy, such transformation will occur not because we understand those experiences but because we are able to embody them in our lives.

Worship experiences do seek to offer us answers to the questions about what our lives in this universe mean. For some religious traditions, the meaning is best understood through a defining narrative, such as the life and death of Jesus Christ. For others a singular story is not enough. The meaning is experienced as invisible to the eye, but resonant in our hearts. In both cases, the practice of liturgy is critical to tell the story or open the heart. The Abbot of Zen Mountain Monastery, John Daido Loori, says that the purpose of liturgy is "to make the invisible, visible."

We Covenant Together

Despite the continuing evidence of Unitarian Universalist worship's roots in Protestant Christian liturgical traditions, there is a critical difference between the meaning of UU worship and the meaning understood by other traditions with Protestant identities. It is the difference between worship founded on covenant and worship founded on creeds. This distinction is crucial for our free faith, and answers basic questions about why and how we gather. In his adult curriculum for new members, Rev. Brent Smith states the theological difference succinctly:

> In orthodox understanding of religious community, creeds like the Apostle's Creed define the center of the church. Theology "begins" with the nature of God because human nature is known (it is essentially depraved or sinful). The most important question is, "What is right belief?" When someone asks, "What does your church believe?" they are asking a question from an orthodox view. It looks back to a time when truth was revealed. Its emphasis is on conforming to a consistent, communal understanding of religion (God, Jesus, morality, etc.) and communal norms regarding faith. Consent involves consenting to place oneself under the theological discipline of seeking to understand and adhere to the church's proclamations of belief. Therefore, the basis of community is an individual's submission to right belief regarding God, as the church has come to know it.
>
> In the Free Church understanding of religion, covenant is prominent. Theology "begins" with the question of human nature, because the nature of God is unknown, each individual having a different and uniquely direct relationship with God. The most important question is, "How do I treat my neighbor, that is, others?" When someone asks, "What does your church do for and in the world?" they are asking a question from a free religious, or liberal religious, view. It looks ahead to a future because truth unfolds. Its emphasis is on personal integrity and an individual's understanding of the religious, and on the

development of an individual's faith. Consent is always operative and always shaping the individual because the freedom to explore and understand one's unique and direct relationship with God is the purpose and aim of spiritual community, of giving one's consent to walk with others. Therefore, the basis of a community is an individual's faithfulness to and with others during life, conceived of as a spiritual walk with others.

Covenants are affirmed in our worship because they represent the foundation upon which our understanding of the church rests. Books such as *Walking Together* by Conrad Wright and *Redeeming Time* by Walter Herz have revisited the covenantal foundations of our congregational polity, as have UUA leadership and training resources that offer guidance on using covenantal processes to strengthen congregational life. If UU congregations are bound together primarily by the promises we make to each other, rather than by creeds we affirm together, then there is much to commend the routine use of a carefully chosen or composed statement of covenant in worship.

We claim no supernatural authority for the covenants we use in our worship. They are not scriptural texts or creedal statements that claim divine origins or sanctions. They have not been passed down from an ecclesiastical hierarchy that claims to represent divine authority. Our covenants come instead from the hearts and minds of our people. They may have been composed and introduced into worship by ministers; they may have been created by lay leaders, individually or through a group process. Some have been affirmed by a congregational vote; others have become a tradition of congregational life through usage.

As we visited evangelical Protestant congregations, we were struck by how noncreedal their worship is becoming. While these congregations may follow a membership intake and formation process that is powerfully creedal, we need to be careful about viewing all of Protestant worship as defined by their creedal platform. The congregationally based United Church of Christ and the Disciples of Christ are covenantal traditions. The Baptist and Pentecostal traditions have never featured creedal confession as a prominent aspect of their worship lives. Instead, these traditions have focused on personal testimony of transformed lives as the best statement of what the church believes and means for its members.

Among the congregations we visited was Vineyard Community Church near Cincinnati. We seated ourselves high in the balcony of a sanctuary larger than many concert halls. The high-energy, pop-praise music worship unfolding below us was augmented by a ceremony we had not yet seen at any of the evangelical services we had attended: a baptism.

Vineyard churches use full immersion baptism in a pool of water built into the chancel area. Even at a distance from the ritual, we were struck by the fact that it was not the minister who proclaimed the believers baptized and saved; it was the person or people who had been most important in introducing them to the Christian way of life. Their use of digital projection capabilities also made an impression on us. As people were escorted into the pool and immersed, there was an accompanying video in which each spoke about what their conversion and baptism meant to them.

Although there was no commonly spoken creed, we were aware that this congregation believed that lives are transformed by the encounter with the Christ and the God they praised, and they held up those testimonials as evidence of both their creed and their covenant.

What we fail to do frequently enough in our UU churches is illustrate the power of our covenants with opportunities in worship for members to testify to the difference their membership commitments have made in their lives. The covenants we use in worship are maps of the same territory we cover in our Unitarian Universalist Purposes and Principles, and in our congregational statements of mission and vision. They are liturgical responses to questions about what we are doing when we worship and why our people come to worship; where we find life's most important salvific meanings; and how we respond to those meanings in worship and daily living.

In a paper on style in liberal worship, prepared for the Prairie Group in 2002, Rev. Roy Philips points us towards five meanings around which we may covenant through our worship:

- We share a common human journey, and so we covenant to value what is common among us over what separates and divides us.

- Each of us has unique dignity and gifts, and so we covenant to recognize and celebrate the dignity and gifts among us in the common life we share.

- We have a responsibility to envision and create a better world, and so we covenant to support and encourage our individual and common efforts towards its attainment.

- Despite the mystery that surrounds our ultimate destiny as a human race, our lives are worthy of praise, and so we covenant to help each other engage the mystery with praise.

- Religion is a human response to the mysterious otherness we encounter in our lives, and so we covenant to cultivate and explore the religious response among us as a defining and ennobling activity of the human race.

To summarize, we covenant to value our common journey, to recognize and respect our individual dignity and gifts, to support the attainment of a better world, to praise the mystery, and to engage in the practices of a religious life.

We encourage any congregation engaging in mission/covenant work that will affect its worship life to explore each of these components, because congregational life is diminished if all five are not present. We would also contend that transformative Unitarian Universalist worship will find ways to hold up in the service stories of how lives have been changed for the better by being bound by these covenants.

The Community of Common Worship

Despite ever-changing theological opinions and shifting theological majorities within our congregations, Unitarians and Universalists and Unitarian Universalists have worshipped together in the presence of the holy, bound together by our covenants on this continent for more than two centuries. We have a common denominator of understanding that worship is done in community. Increasingly we understand that while individuals may have private spiritual devotional practices, and individuals and groups may have mystical experiences of awe, wonder, and beauty, these are not worship. Worship is a communal and intentional event, constructed from the building blocks of the liturgical arts and intended to be practiced over time.

Our most widely understood definition of worship, cited by theistic and nontheistic UUs alike, seems to be: We gather together to hold up those things of ultimate worth, meaning, and value. It follows from this definition that any elements arranged in any order or form that calls to mind things of ultimate meaning and value should work as a component of our worship. We lack a common understanding about the value and meaning and the power of liturgy, which we would define as: the artful and intentional creation of devotional and inspirational experiences intended to transform the self. ✓

The covenantal foundation of our Unitarian Universalist worship tradition handicaps our ability to appreciate the way liturgy sustains the community of common worship. We come from the American Congregational Puritan tradition, and although most Unitarian Universalists would have a hard time describing how our Puritan ancestry influences our worship today, it undoubtedly does. Our Puritan heritage is rooted in the Calvinist conviction that the key sacrament in worship is the interpretation of the word of God, found in the Scriptures. Although we have transcended the Calvinist understanding of where Scripture can be found and what its interpretation means, we continue to be People of the Book and ✓ People of the Word. Most of our members believe that the holy will truly be found in the sermon, first of all, and in the literal prose of the readings and affirmations heard and spoken. This belief contributes to minimizing our interest in the other liturgical arts: music, hymn and song, poetry, ritual, dance, and drama.

Our evident aversion to icons also stems from our Puritan heritage. The simplicity that was part of the Puritans' faith has influenced our architecture and our attitudes towards aesthetics. As inheritors of the Protestant reaction to Roman Catholic symbolism, and as people who believe that redemption comes from personal experiences of insight and grace rather than the offices and rites of the church, we are skeptical of the power of icons, symbols, and rituals. Exploring them feels like a betrayal.

At West Shore Church, we are reminded of this Puritan influence each week when we gaze at the large, usually empty wall behind our pulpit. While at times this wall has been decorated with commissioned art or other temporary artistic innovations, the majority of our church's members feel comfortable with the emptiness of that space. One person told us that it gives her permission to fill it with whatever is going on in her body and mind in response to the service.

We were intrigued with how the congregation might respond to an opportunity to purchase and permanently mount a digital projector in the sanctuary ceiling, allowing us to project images, hymns, and words onto the empty wall during services. Many members donated to a special fund set up to make the projector possible. Those who expressed concern largely responded to the frequency of projected images, rather than the validity of using them at all. We believe that the impermanence of the projected images and hymns, and discretion in their use, minimized any outcry that the empty wall was being overthrown as an element of our worship space.

Our aversion to rituals and symbols has reinforced our noncreedal stance with regard to both membership and worship. We have an underlying fear of creeping creedalism. Many of our members see fixed symbols placed on the walls or experienced through rituals and ceremonies in very literal ways that fail to appreciate the flexible metaphorical possibilities for the meanings they might contain.

There is one more element of our UU tradition that comes from our Puritan ancestry: our powerful belief in our first Source.

Contained in our 1985 UUA Statement of Purposes and Principles, this Source is the "direct experience of transcending mystery and wonder." ✓ We believe that the individual apprehension of the holy is the first wellspring of religious life. It doesn't come from any traditional single source like a holy book or a founding teacher, and it doesn't come through collective devotional or spiritual practice. The emphasis on the individual in that first Source overwhelms all the other Sources we claim, which arise from collective rather than individual experience. When we view our worship life primarily through the lens of the first Source, minimizing the influence of historic traditions and their *must* liturgical expression, we risk treating worship as thinly disguised self-improvement. ✓

Despite the fact that we will never rest our faith on a foundation represented by a single holy book or prophet, our liturgy has the potential to share a critical common characteristic with the liturgical traditions of other world faiths: Our worship life tells a saving story. Our task as worship leaders is to exegete that story, and weave together the threads of our tradition in weekly works of art that tell us how to live a Unitarian Universalist religious life. The liberal religious tradition and way of life is not circumscribed by our Judeo-Christian heritage, yet that is the strongest of the threads that we follow back through time. It is woven with others into a tapestry of sources and possibilities, but there is no question in our minds that our congregational life resonates most strongly with the church forms, language, and culture of Protestant Christianity. The culture and traditions of a congregation's life are critical in shaping their worship.

The Role of Culture and Tradition

Early in our travels, we stopped for a couple of days to visit with colleagues in Maryland. Sitting in a coffee shop outside of Adelphia, they asked whether we planned to primarily visit Unitarian Universalist churches. We explained that we would be visiting some UU churches, but we were also looking for services that were more cutting edge.

Our colleagues looked at us with wry amusement. "Good luck," said one of them, as he picked up his guitar, heading off to church to practice music for Sunday with other church members, "but I think you'll be surprised to discover that we UUs are actually one of the more liturgically innovative denominations out there."

His comment stayed with us, and every time we attended church in a UU congregation new to us, we realized that we needed to ask ourselves (with as little prejudgment as possible): Where did this church's worship life come from? How had it transformed its participants' lives for the better? What would a cutting-edge innovation for this church look like and would it make the experience better?

We had assumed, and quickly confirmed, that compared to evangelical churches, most of our congregations do not offer as many dimensions in the range of worship opportunities. Often we provide a one-dimensional experience: a single service that has to fit all ages, sizes, and cultural preferences. Most of our worship elements engage one locus of religious understanding—the mind—and only minimally touch the body, the heart, and the spirit. One kind of music has, until recently, been predominant: classical, rather than jazz, folk, pop, or rock. Our worship relies on one sensory mode—sound—rather than sight, smell, or touch. This is not to say that one-dimensional worship is inevitably bad, or that we didn't find other traditions with a one-dimensional approach; we did, although they may operate from a different baseline of religious understanding, music, and sensory stimuli than we do. However, whatever the baseline of its elements might be, one-dimensional worship is worship that fails to live up to its full potential.

There are important reasons why our UU worship life remains one-dimensional. Nearly half of our congregations have under one hundred attending worship and almost a third are lay led. More than half the congregations that have ministers are "pastoral-sized" churches (between 50 and 150 members), led by an older, humanist-oriented membership with inherent conservative tendencies when it comes to moving beyond sermon-centered worship with a classical music baseline. Sermon-centered worship is in our DNA as a religious movement with its roots in the Puritan congregational tradition.

These observations about our church suggest that the dimensions of worship—the ability of the service to engage mind, heart, body, and spirit, to touch all the senses, to appeal to diverse generations and cultures—arise from something beyond the will and creativity of the worship leader. We believe that there are four dynamic forces that influence how a congregation worships, and these forces are often beyond the control of the worship leaders to directly influence in a short period of time. They include the founding culture of the congregation, the worship traditions the church embraces or respects, the musical baseline that the church accepts as normative for worship, and the size of the space available for worship.

Of these four, the founding culture is the most difficult to describe because it can be a unique and subtle aspect to identify and track over time. It's a big component of a congregation's DNA. (See "Qualities of Transformative Worship.") Before we visited Saddleback Community Church, we read *The Purpose-Driven Church,* the best-selling book written by their founding pastor Rick Warren. We recognized that this congregation was a brand-new entrepreneurial start with its founding pastor and culture still intact and extremely visible. This visibility has made a tremendous difference in its ability to create an innovative worship model that has transformed its members' lives and the shape of American worship.

Even though Pastor Warren defined and controlled the founding culture of Saddleback, he is also a product of a Southern Baptist tradition that believes that the preached word of God as expressed in the Bible is the heart of the worship experience. This is a particular tradition of worship, which (despite its innovations) the Saddleback service respected and embodied. Within the diversity of worship experiences they offered each weekend, all participants heard the same sermon video-feed to their worship venue.

One of Saddleback's primary insights was that people might be attracted to come to church in greater numbers if they heard the kind of music they enjoy listening to on their drive to work. Warren redefined the baseline for church music, realizing that the musical style of a worship service has a crucial influence on its feel.

Finally, as Saddleback grew in size, the congregation was able to adapt technology to accommodate the largest worship service they wanted, and at the same time re-create smaller venues to accommodate the various cultural niches in their larger congregation.

The four forces that influence worship are important in understanding not only the largest, most innovative evangelical congregations, but also the smallest and most traditional congregations. In Jacksonville, Florida, Kathleen visited a Haitian Baptist church that was founded about the same time as Saddleback, but was quite different. This church respected some of the same Baptist worship traditions that influenced Saddleback's services. The center of their worship was the preached word of God revealed in the Bible; they also shared similar understandings of the meaning of the Christian message. However, the founding culture of this congregation, rooted in the experience of Haitian immigrants to Florida, was quite different from the culture of the Southern California suburban founders of Saddleback. The music they brought with them and the ways they played and sang created a different baseline. The economic resources available to this congregation to build a church that could house their worship could not match the resources of the Saddleback members. As a result, these two Christian services felt very different.

We see these same kinds of differences in the worship styles of Unitarian Universalist congregations, even those that share the same geographic region. These differences have to do with the ways the four forces interact. During our visit to Dallas, we learned about two neighboring UU congregations with different worship styles: Horizon Unitarian Universalist Church, now in Carrollton, and Pathways Church, now in Southlake, Texas. These congregations shared certain traditions of UU congregational worship, and they both shared some of the same founding culture associated with First Unitarian Church in Dallas and the northern suburbs of the Dallas area. They both had a single lead minister who influenced the founding culture of the congregation. Their worship experiences were different, however, because of some key distinctions. Horizon began as a lay-led congregation and had its first year of services without a settled minister. Pathways opened as a minister-led congregation. The congregations had different musical baselines. Horizon was influenced by the interests and skills of its first settled minister, Rev. Dennis Hamilton, to offer music that went beyond traditional UU hymnody to include bluegrass, folk, and gospel. Pathways' first minister, Rev. Anthony David, wanted from the beginning to try electric music as the congregation's baseline, with original UU praise songs and inclusive praise music from other sources. Horizon began slowly, adapting its worship style to the shopping mall space it rented for seven years before its members were able to build their own worship space. Pathways had a vision of growing quickly and wanted to try the style of worship that works for larger congregations. However, the rented space they acquired was not well suited to that model of service. The forces came together differently in these two neighboring congregations to create some of the conditions of worship culture that a minister or worship leader must work with.

Neither Horizon nor Pathways had any desire to re-create the worship service style at their founding congregation, First Unitarian Church of Dallas. They each offered a recognizable UU service that was nonetheless unique. If these two suburban congregations were to experience a growth curve that led them towards the size of First Unitarian Church of Dallas (over one thousand members) their founding cultures, the traditions they had developed, their musical baselines, and the changes of population in the suburbs they served would all influence how their worship evolved to fill larger worship spaces.

Despite their differences, an element these two neighboring congregations shared was the belief that worship is primary to the purpose of congregational life, and that worship is the central spiritual practice that Unitarian Universalist congregations offer their members. These were both critical components of their philosophy and strategy for growth. They are what our most vibrant and successful congregations have in common with the megachurches and the new emergent churches that are evolving in counterpoint to these large evangelical congregations.

The Emergent Church

When we started our sabbatical research and travels, we both believed that we would find the vanguard of worship life in the large evangelical churches. We were especially interested in what we could learn about contemporary and praise worship and how we could use these forms in a Unitarian Universalist context. What we found instead was that the most exciting and creative work in worship and liturgy was being done in "emergent churches"—smaller evangelical and mainline congregations offering services that attract younger adults into explorations of older worship forms in new ways. The seeker service worship involving praise songs, prayer, and lengthy sermons had begun to feel as dated to many younger Christians as the traditional Protestant hymnody, responsive prayers, and sermons in the mainline churches their parents attended.

A light bulb turned on over our heads when we realized that younger evangelicals and mainline Christians were discovering and experimenting with older traditional worship forms, and reinventing them in innovative ways. They were discovering that worship could have new depth for them as a spiritual practice, encouraging them towards greater commitment in their faith, not only to evangelism, but also to a life of integrity, service, and devotion. One name that turned up regularly in our Internet and literature searches under "emergent church" was the Cedar Ridge Community Church in Spencerville Maryland, led by Rev. Brian McLaren, its founding pastor.

On our way to Washington, D.C. from Philadelphia, we realized that we were not far from Cedar Ridge, and we called to see if anyone would be available to talk to us. The staff member who answered our call told us the pastor had left the building, in more ways than one. The interest in his work had made him much in demand as a church consultant and he had transitioned to a new senior pastor role that no longer involved routine responsibility for the operation of the church.

However, we were very fortunate to be directed to one of the most engaging worship leaders we found during our entire sabbatical, Betsy Mitchell-Henning, director of liturgical arts at Cedar Ridge. Betsy was welcoming and generous with her time, telling us the story of Cedar Ridge Church and its philosophy of worship, showing us their worship space, and describing the ways that her role had evolved. We found Betsy at the mixing board in the sanctuary working on sound and video for next week's service. Her spiky red-black hair, jewelry, and tattoos did not match any stereotypes for a director of liturgical arts in any evangelical church we knew. Neither did the worship that she had assisted the Cedar Ridge Worship team in creating.

When we dropped in on Cedar Ridge Church, it was twenty-five years old. It had begun in Rev. McLaren's apartment and was originally based on the Willow Creek model of excellent preaching and a multimedia liturgy that could rival television. At the time of our visit, they saw themselves as having moved in a different direction from Willow Creek, by emphasizing more participatory worship and a commitment to church life as a spiritual practice engaged with the world. They also stood out as an evangelical Christian church with many liberal social values, including an understated but clearly welcoming attitude to gay and lesbian parishioners. The theological and social spectrum of people attending Cedar Ridge rivaled the diversity in UU churches, but they were still a largely white church in a suburban neighborhood that had a lot of ethnic diversity.

Cedar Ridge grew out of the Community Church (Baptist) in the College Park, Maryland, area. For ten years they met in high school auditoriums. By 1995, they had bought a historic farm and by 1998 moved onto the property and into their own new worship facility. Their facility was in auditorium style, with classrooms off all the surrounding hallways. It was intended for multiple uses: worship, social events, youth activities, weddings, banquets, etc. They had completed a renovation of the barn on the property for use as a youth ministry and program building. As of 2006, they had fewer than five hundred members, but their worship attendance each Sunday was higher than their stated membership, exactly the opposite of most mainline Protestant churches.

When we visited, Cedar Ridge hosted two services, one at 9:00 and the other at 11:00; both services were the same. They had about 250 in worship at the first service, and about 350 in the second. Their sanctuary had moveable chairs, and a center platform surrounded by seating on three sides. There was no pulpit. Preaching happened from the platform, and the preacher was free to move around the congregation. Behind the platform was a table with votive candles and a decorative holder that could hold many candles. Behind this was a standard stage where the worship band played. On either side of the stage were two angled white walls that were painted with a special paint for projected images. The sanctuary could seat as many as seven hundred in a standard and crowded theater-style arrangement. The room as we saw it was set for four hundred people.

Around the sanctuary were several stations marked by banners for prayer, offering, and communion. The space was otherwise without adornment, with a simple wooden cross on the central table. Despite using some of the Willow Creek/Saddleback formula for music and preaching, Cedar Ridge went in an entirely different direction by reclaiming some of the older worship practices of the Orthodox and Anglo-Catholic traditions. During the communion ritual, the congregation engaged in one or more of several choices for personal devotional practice. One involved receiving communion from the minister, although communion could also be taken privately at one of the worship stations along the walls or, with a group of family and friends, shared around one of the tables set up in corners of the sanctuary for that purpose. Worshipers could also engage in private prayer or meditation accompanied by music. They could engage in lighting devotional or commemorative candles. Alternatively, they could meet with a minister or worship leader to make prayer requests or pray.

Betsy described herself as a former Episcopalian, who came to Cedar Ridge in 1991 looking for a church that combined both the incarnational qualities of Anglo-Catholic worship and the powerful preaching of the Protestant style. She was clearly a person with more liberal social values than the right-wing views held by most evangelicals, and Cedar Ridge reflected such a mix. They were clearly an evangelical church on the "left hand of God," to use Rabbi Michael Lerner's phrase.

We found ourselves both excited and challenged by the emergent church movement, and by the style of this particular church. Cedar Ridge by no means defines the forms of worship being practiced in emergent churches. These forms include independent entrepreneurial congregations primarily serving young adult populations, new church plants started by established evangelical churches who give them independent authority for designing a different style of service, and established churches whose leadership culture has envisioned a new way of worship based in Christian retraditioning. What all the forms have in common is a flexible post-modern creativity reminiscent of what Unitarian Universalism has always claimed as a defining characteristic.

The freedom in Unitarian Universalism has always invited experimentation and adaptation of traditional forms. This has been one of our attractions to seekers who call themselves spiritual but not religious, which turns out to be territory that a generation of younger Christians is now exploring. The worship lives and worship services of these individuals are becoming more creative, more participatory, more accessible, and more explicit about worship as a primary spiritual practice. Worship as spiritual practice is hardly a new understanding. In our travels, we saw it frequently named as an important dimension of congregational life in thriving mainline churches. We realized that the performance aspect of evangelical megachurch worship and the passivity it engenders in the worshiping congregation has begun to disenchant this new generation of evangelicals.

In the Unitarian Universalist churches we visited, we found fewer people in the pews who were articulate about understanding worship as spiritual practice. On the contrary, a significant amount of the current writing about worship, and a great deal of the conversation we had with our colleagues during the sabbatical travels, was about worship as a focus of conflict in a congregation, rather than as a cherished commonly held spiritual practice. At the end of our first month of traveling, we discovered a church consultant whose writing on churches of intentional practice helped us better understand why worship has the potential to become a congregational war zone.

When a congregation experiences conflict over traditions or innovations in worship, it is because they are conflicted about who they are or who they want to become. In her book *The Practicing Congregation*, Diana Butler Bass comments:

> To outsiders, arguments over worship may seem trivial. However, they are not. These arguments are conflicts regarding religious practice, and when properly understood and interpreted, they reveal a much deeper fissure in American spirituality than does the "liberal vs. conservative" framework. Such conflicts expose a practice continuum—an often-invisible field of expectations, style, and activities. The practice continuum exists in many mainline congregations as these churches struggle between the poles of established and intentional churchgoing.

Intentional churchgoing involves seeing worship as the primary spiritual practice that informs everything else a person does in the church. Intentional churchgoers believe that participating in church life has the power to transform their lives towards greater depth, joy, and meaning. Intentional church life engages members in a community that sees itself as more than a civic institution or club or school; that sees itself as a continuing embodiment of a religious way of life and tradition. That way of life is revealed in stories, images, music, and metaphors that speak of ethical imperatives and incarnated truths. It is revealed in worship.

As we visited several more congregations identified with the emergent church movement, we began to understand that the shift they represented was not just a change in how these younger evangelicals viewed the possibilities and the promise of their worship life: It was a change from established to intentional churchgoing. No doubt the founders of the megachurch movement represented the same kind of shift when they started these congregations in homes, drive-ins, movie theaters, and storefronts. As their model for doing church has become the prototype for evangelical congregations, the inability of these churches to sustain creativity and intimacy within these formulaic structures has created the passion for more intentional churchgoing among emergent church leaders.

Where is that passion for intentional churchgoing in Unitarian Universalism? Where is our emergent church? Newcomers unfamiliar with spiritual practice as a regular part of life rarely find explicit instruction about how to think about the worship experience as spiritual practice. Longtime UU members, particularly those uncomfortable with traditional religious language, balk at the idea that their church attendance is spiritual practice. They come for the intellectual stimulation of the sermon, they say, or for the community, or for the religious education classes for their children.

The truth, however, is that attendance at worship is the primary and often the only explicit spiritual practice that many Unitarian Universalists undertake. If the members of our congregations are not approaching their worship life with passion, the ministers fail to do so at their peril. In passionately describing how this realization made a difference in his own ministry, Rev. Tom Schade of First Unitarian Church of Worcester, Massachusetts, said to us: "If worship is their primary spiritual practice, then I'd better be fully present when I am leading worship." Being fully present means being able to take every moment of the worship service seriously, to plan it thoroughly, to engage with it fully, and to value each part of the service as critical to this life-changing practice.

QUALITIES OF
TRANSFORMATIVE WORSHIP

On a Sunday in late July, we pulled into a gas station in downtown Denver. That morning we had attended worship at the Church of Religious Science, an older independent megachurch with a charismatic founder whose successor was trying to reinvent the church's worship and message for a new generation. Earlier that week we had attended an emergent church attracting the younger crowd that the Religious Science folks wished they would draw. Later that evening we were going to visit another emergent church, called Scum of the Earth, which met in an abandoned grocery store and served urban youth who came to church in goth and grunge, excited to hear loud punk rock praise music and long sermons.

While at the gas station, a taxi pulled into a nearby parking spot. The cab driver got out, went to his trunk, pulled out a rug, and laid it on the ground. His back to the mountains in the west, he began his midday prayer, the *dhuhr*, the second of the five times in every day that Muslims observe a call to prayer.

For all our frantic study of worship that week, and for all the worship services we had attended in Denver, this was one aspect of worship life we had not yet touched upon: the way that corporate worship is reinforced by personal devotional practice. Here, in the middle of this busy gas station, we witnessed one man's private prayer to his God, a prayer shared at the same time of day in Denver by thousands of Muslims. As we pulled away from the gas station, we both felt as if we too, had been in church, in the presence of the Unseen, if only for a moment.

It was for us a different kind of transformative moment, but one that resonated with our recent experiences in formal services. We were lifted up out of the ordinary into an extraordinary moment of worship. That's what we were looking for on our travels throughout the country—a moment in and out of time, when we felt the presence of something larger.

Liberal religious worship informed by the Protestant congregational tradition is offered in thousands of congregations all over the world every week. In some places it is instrumental in changing for the better the lives of those who share it. Sometimes it is transformative worship, changing the wafers and grape juice of everyday life into the body and blood of a life redeemed from meaninglessness, materialism, and numbness. Sometimes it happens because of one service that is remembered for a lifetime. More often it happens slowly, service after service, the way that rivers, rain, and wind shape a mountain landscape. It happens because participation in a religious community and in corporate worship involve people in personal devotional practice outside their congregations, which makes a difference in how they live their lives at work, in their families, and in their private experiences. This is what it means for worship to "work," to be transformative.

Transformative worship should be understood as the primary common spiritual practice of Unitarian Universalists, and as a critical engine that can drive Unitarian Universalist growth. This cannot happen unless this common spiritual practice also starts to affect the ways that Unitarian Universalists lead their lives outside of church. One way to think about a worship service is that each of its elements points toward spiritual practices in which we might engage throughout the week.

Throughout our ministries and during our sabbatical experiences, we tried to deepen our understanding of transformative worship by first monitoring and appreciating our own reactions to worship experiences. That's why this concentrated time in other churches' pews was so valuable. Each week, we would talk together about how the worship we had experienced made a difference in our day, our week, our lives. Rereading the notes of our conversations on the road, we found that transformative worship:

- invites the congregation into holy time and creates sacred space from the very beginning of the service

- includes an affirmation of the congregation's central mission, values, and promises

- uses powerful symbols that are familiar to the congregation and are rooted in the community's history and tradition

- is culturally sensitive, honoring and interpreting the context and setting of ritual elements and service content drawn from the world's diverse cultures

- finds ways to invite and include people at all ages and stages of life

- skillfully uses the arts, particularly music, to express the ineffable in ways that are culturally accessible to the congregation

- recognizes inclusive singing as a way of opening the heart to the presence of the holy and to the mission, vision, and values of the congregation

- uses any announcements as a reminder of the mission, vision, and values of the congregation, and as a bridge from the service to personal actions and commitments

- invites and creates congregations of generosity and abundance

- finds ways to recognize individual lives within the body of the community, holding the personal and the collective in dynamic tension

- includes silence and words that remind us of our dependency on the mystery of life and each other

- honors traditional and contemporary sources for the congregation's faith journey and helps place this journey in time, through the framework of the liturgical year

- can happen without a sermon, but the power of the word through excellent preaching is the key that unlocks the possibility of transformation in most of our congregations

35

- sends people out into the world with a personal sense of mission, with their highest values reinforced

We believe that each part of a worship service contains a transformational element that the service as a whole embodies. We earlier noted that church growth consultants have used the metaphor of DNA to convey the idea that a new congregation's central mission, values, and culture must be intentionally established before public worship begins. This missional DNA must then be evident in everything the congregation does, in every ministry and meeting, and especially in its worship. We believe that a congregation's worship life is built on this DNA and can see evidence of it in each component of the worship service. Examining and understanding the way you worship can be a vehicle for "genetic research" into a congregation's identity. Changing the way you worship can be the vehicle for changing the congregation's DNA towards a new identity that its members envision and desire.

Entering into Holy Time

It was ten minutes to eleven, and we were lost. We thought we knew how to get to All Souls Church in Washington, D.C. from the Beltway, but clearly we'd missed a turn somewhere. We knew that by the time we found the church and parked we would be cutting our arrival time very close to the beginning of the processional, and the processional at All Souls should not be missed.

There were many aspects of the worship at All Souls Church, Unitarian, in 2005 that had attracted our attention and been a factor in the church's growth since 2001. Most important was the leadership and preaching of Rev. Robert Hardies, but the role of worship producer assumed by Music Director John Strang has also been a significant part of the compelling worship services that happen there every week.

Of particular interest to us was the way the congregation enters into worship. They begin with a pealing of bells from their bell tower, an element that is listed in the order of service as their beginning point for worship. They follow this with the chalice lighting. When we interviewed Rob and John, they told us: "With the lighting of the chalice we are called to silence in preparation for the music for meditation. The purpose of this practice is two-fold. First, it calms the chaos of what's happening outside the sanctuary so that people prepare themselves to be in a space for worship. Secondly, it leads nicely into the music for meditation."

The order of service reads: "During the music for meditation, all are invited to come forward to light a candle of joy or concern from the chalice flame. At the sounding of the chime, the congregation rises." The music can be an organ selection from John Strang or a piece from a jazz artist in residence.

When the selection ends, the organ introduces the processional hymn. Each week, the choir, liturgists, service participants, and minister begin the service with a processional down the center aisle to a hymn. They have a collection of processional hymns that most of the congregation now knows by heart. Hardies and Strang described for us the value of a collection of six to eight regularly used hymns: By memorizing this music the congregation "owns" the processional. The opening parts of the service lead up to this early climactic moment that signals the congregation's entry into holy time. They have heard the bells calling them to church, they have ignited the symbol of the faith community, and they have brought the cares of their lives to mind and laid them on the altar. The meditative music helps them let those cares go, so that worship can begin.

Often the procession is accompanied by African drums or some other kind of percussion instrument. The choir usually remains on the main floor after the processional, a change from earlier years when they were most often in the loft. The processional ends, and the worship leader goes to the pulpit and offers the call to worship.

We know that most of the readers of this book worship in congregations that do not have the rich history, traditions, and resources of All Souls Church. However, we also know that most of the worship order and innovations we have described from our experience at All Souls can be introduced in a congregation of any size.

The difference in All Souls' worship was not resources, but attention and creativity. They paid attention to how they entered holy time, and they were creative in blending the elements of entry to create a true emotional and spiritual gateway into worship.

There was a time in UU worship that many of our congregations would avoid using terms such as *Invocation* or *Call to Worship* to begin the service, because we knew we did not agree on what we were invoking or worshipping. As we traveled throughout our association of congregations, we had a distinct feeling that those days are past. Although it is true that Unitarian Universalists don't share a common theology of the divine, we share a passion for apprehending the holy and celebrating the mystery in which we live. This is what we must invoke when we gather for our common worship each week: the recognition and creation of holy time and space, where we can encounter the spirit of life, that invisible fountain which bubbles up within our lives and in the world around us, quenching our thirst for beauty and meaning.

If the purpose of liturgy is "to make the invisible, visible," the invisible realities that are present when we gather for worship must be invoked, invited, and embodied from the very beginning of a service. Some of the invocation is created by the aesthetics of the space. Unitarian Universalist worship spaces range from a Gothic cathedral design to a rented elementary-school cafeteria. While every space has fixed architectural aspects, we still have creative control over many elements that make the entry into holy time possible. Banners, altar flowers, art pieces, and symbols all can be arranged to remind us that this space has been set aside for this time for a special purpose that deserves our utmost attention and respect.

Beyond these aesthetic elements, our entry into the worship space also includes other emotional and spiritual triggers. We see those known to us and those who are strangers. We see symbols that represent history, authority, and beauty. We see and hear the musicians and music, the words on the printed page and from the lips of the worship leader. Beyond all these tangible signs, there are some invisible elements that require our invocation, some qualities of transformative worship that somehow must be made evident in the course of the service. They include:

- the lineage of spiritual ancestors that are present, the "cloud of witnesses" that made this tradition and congregation possible

- the present-day relationships of love and friendship that would look like a force field of affection if they were all visible

- the convictions of faith, values of the heart, aspirations for the future that are at the heart of this congregation's life

Even to the smallest details, the first visual and auditory impressions of a service are vital in creating a space that allows these elements to reveal themselves. The prelude music, the care taken with seating, and the degree to which the order of service makes us feel comfortable with what is about to happen are all elements that make a difference in how we enter into holy time. The first things that happen in a service must speak to the presence of the holy embodied in the abundance of this scarred creation. If we begin worship with a cheery "Good morning" and a welcome to visitors followed by announcements, it would be fair to assume that at best the community life of the church is what is holy. If, however, that is not the limit of what we can affirm together as holy, we must pay attention to how the service starts and what that calls us to do together.

Affirming Mission, Values and Promises

In a church where one of us served as an interim minister, members each Sunday spoke a covenant composed by James Vila Blake in 1894. Written for a Unitarian congregation in Chicago, Illinois, the covenant read,

> Love is the Spirit of this Church, and service its law.
> This is our great covenant:
> To dwell together in peace, to seek the truth in love,
> And to help one another.

It was part of the fabric of their worship service and not to be changed. But not only was it part of their Sunday morning experience, it had also worked its way into meetings as opening or closing words. Many could speak it from memory. As part of the liturgy, speaking the covenant brought the congregation's attention back to its raison d'etre: to dwell together in peace, seek the truth in love, and help one another. Over time, the weekly unison reading of the covenant created the feeling that this was a "safe" congregation—that the members knew why it existed, and had a clear command of how people were to be in relationship with one another.

Reciting a regular covenant is one way that a congregation affirms its central mission, purpose, and values early in its worship service. The signage on the church building, the displays on the walls, and the text of the order of service all provide additional affirmation from the very beginning of the total experience of attending worship.

During our sabbatical journey, our experiences reminded us how first-time visitors to a congregation are often ill at ease. They don't know what to expect. They know few or none of the people attending the service. They are worried about whether the philosophical or theological expressions of the congregation might make them uncomfortable. People need to feel secure in their expectations before engaging fully with the worship service. We found that the congregations whose worship had a visible or early expression of their identity were the congregations that helped us to easily engage with the worship experience. Although we may not have agreed theologically with their point of view, at least we knew what the church stood for. Used liturgically, covenantal statements reveal a congregation's identity, which in turn, helps to make the service more accessible.

Covenants can also serve another purpose. The weekly speaking or hearing of the church's covenant can anchor its members in tradition that can be passed down from generation to generation. Covenants thus can provide the link between our Unitarian Universalist past, a congregation's present, and our children's future commitment "to dwell together in peace, to seek the truth in love, and to help one another."

According to the 2004 survey of UU congregational worship conducted by the Commission on Appraisal (COA), which drew responses from 370 congregations, fewer than half of them regularly use covenants as an element of their liturgy. This may seem a surprisingly low figure for congregations whose polity is rooted in covenantal theology. Nevertheless, the survey findings demonstrate that covenants rank among the most widely used liturgical elements in Unitarian Universalist worship, lagging behind only sermons, hymns, readings, joys and concerns, and chalice lightings. In comparison to more orthodox Protestant traditions, we use covenants in worship far more frequently than we use communion liturgies, doxologies, responsive readings, or litanies.

The Blake Covenant ranks among the oldest continuously used covenants among us and is spoken weekly today by about a quarter of the congregations that responded to the worship survey. One reason for its popularity is that even the youngest children capable of memorization can have a relationship with its meaning. It begins with the word *love*, one of the most powerful emotions humans can know and something every child treasures or longs for. Helping is another concept that is easy for the youngest church member to grasp, because help is part of everyday life for children. Even if the word *service* is a little abstract and might get confused with church service, the commitment to "help one another" reminds us that being of service to others and to the world is a central tenet of our religious life.

Another popular covenant among Unitarian Universalists was written by the Universalist minister L. Griswold Williams, and published in 1933 in his compilation "Antiphonal Readings for Free Worship." The Williams Covenant has equal currency with the Blake Covenant according to the 2004 worship survey, with about a quarter of the responding congregations reporting its use. Entitled "A Covenant for Free Worship," it reads,

> Love is the doctrine of this church,
> The quest for truth is its sacrament,
> And service is its prayer.

> To dwell together in peace,
> To seek knowledge in freedom,
> To serve human need,
> To the end that all souls shall grow into harmony
> with the Divine–
> Thus do we covenant with each other and with God.

Both covenants are used with variations from congregation to congregation. Indeed, this spirit of creative adaptation of liturgical elements to suit the theological or aesthetic tastes of congregations or worship leaders is very common among us. Another quarter of the congregations responding to the COA survey reported that the covenant they used was locally written, often reflecting their statement of mission and purpose. Whatever the source of the covenantal liturgy, what is most important is that the congregation routinely affirms what is most central about who they are and why they are together.

The Power of Symbols

During our respective ministries we've both spoken with members of our congregations who had recently visited a certain Unitarian Universalist church in another city. Our parishioners had good things to say about the other church and its service, but we were each struck by one recurrent reaction that could be summed up in three words: Where's the chalice?

This reaction is testimony to the ubiquity and power that the flaming chalice as a symbol of Unitarian Universalism has attained in the last half century. It is also testimony to some confusion about how, when, and why symbols and rituals become a part of Unitarian Universalist worship. Unfortunately, we do not have a reliable statistic to illustrate the ubiquity of the chalice symbol. Due to a proofreading error, the 2004 survey instrument used by the Commission on Appraisal did not include "chalice lighting" among the checklist of worship elements that congregations were requested to report. Despite the omission, 59 percent of the reporting congregations either specifically wrote in "chalice lighting" or sent sample orders of service that included it as a regular element. If a response had been requested, no doubt the number of congregations reporting its use would have been much higher. Our personal guess would be 90 percent or more. This response rate means that chalice lightings rank with hymns, songs and readings from UUA-published hymnals, announcements, and joys and concerns as the most commonly used liturgical elements in our services.

Although lighting a chalice is the most widely used ritual in Unitarian Universalist worship, it isn't hard to find congregations that do not include the practice. Most often they are congregations with long and well-defined traditions of worship that preceded the surge in popularity of this symbol. The questions that interested us were these: What transformative role does the chalice lighting play in the service? And for those congregations that do not light a chalice, what other liturgical element performs that transformative role?

A legacy of our Puritan Protestant lineage is the modest usage of symbols, and of rituals surrounding symbols, in worship. Indeed, the trend in twentieth-century Unitarian and Universalist worship prior to and in the decade following the merger was to banish symbols, particularly the cross, from the sanctuary. Many Northeast UU congregations can tell stories of their debates over whether the cross on the wall or altar should be taken down.

Our contemporary use of a flaming chalice symbol originated in 1941 in a design created by Hans Deutsch as a logo for the Unitarian Service Committee's relief efforts during World War II. The chalice symbol resembled the image of the cross, so its use spread slowly among Unitarian congregations. Newer congregations, particularly the many fellowships and churches begun between 1948 and 1962, minimized symbols in their spaces, often opting for abstract artistic creations that were open to interpretation. It was only after the Unitarian Universalist merger prompted an interest in new common symbols that the use of the chalice symbol became more widespread.

The attraction of lighting a chalice as a liturgical addition to services during the 1960s spoke to a deep need emerging from congregations for elements of a common UU identity that could transcend our increasing theological diversity. During the 1950s and 1960s, the primary theological tension in Unitarian Universalism seemed to be between humanists and Christians. After the explosion of Eastern and new age religious exploration in the 1970s, the range of religious practice and theological expression in our congregations became much wider. Theologically identified UU interest groups were created by practicing Buddhists and Jews who were members of UU congregations. Earth-centered and pagan practitioners claimed a place at our theological table in the 1980s and 1990s. The chalice became a common element to include not only in Sunday's common worship but also in the logos and identity-based worship services conducted by these diverse communities.

To identify with a community of faith and practice is a life-transforming decision. Religious identity is a unique component of identity formation that each person can accept, reject, or find anew during a lifetime. It is unique because in most cases it is an identity that invites people to transcend all the particular identities associated with their birth.

The possibilities for the flaming chalice as a component of transformational worship reside in its power as an archetypal symbol of identity. It reminds us that despite the particularities of our congregational lives, we are part of a religious community whose values, practices, and lineage reach deep into the well of human experience. This community is bigger than our own likes and dislikes in worship, bigger than the generational differences among us, bigger than the personalities and ministers that are part of our own congregation, bigger even than the Unitarian Universalist Association as an embodiment of that community.

Some other transformative symbols are used in worship in Unitarian Universalist congregations, but they tend to have an association with that congregation's particular history and traditions or with only particular liturgical seasons or occasions. There is nothing that has emerged in four generations of post-World War II Unitarian Universalism that compares with the flaming chalice as a symbol of both transformation and unity.

Our humanist members are usually the parishioners who claim to have the least interest in symbols and the rituals that surround them, so we were excited about visiting the First Unitarian Society of Minneapolis, a congregation with a proud humanist heritage and identity, and a tradition of excellence in worship. What we didn't expect to carry away from our visit was a beautiful program that focused on the ritual of lighting a chalice as a way of educating and integrating young children into worship.

We brought the program, created by Rev. Kendyl Gibbons, back to West Shore Church and have been delighted to rediscover the wonder of this ritual with our third and fourth graders. Admittedly, the attraction for some of the children is getting to light that flame. The training sessions we offer, however, are an opportunity for us as ministers to revisit the history and meanings contained within the chalice symbol, and what it means for us today, in words that third and fourth graders can appreciate.

We have found no better evidence, or teachers, about the transformative role of the flaming chalice symbol in our services than the children who are our chalice lighters.

Engaging with Cultural Misappropriation

During our sabbatical stay in Fort Worth, Texas, we interviewed Charles Gaby and studied the contemporary worship service he developed at First United Methodist Church. We were so impressed with Charles and his service that we have written his work up in detail in the appendix at the end of this book. He developed the service in concert with Rev. Jim Connor and Rev. Linda McDermott. One element of the service was the lighting of copal, a resin incense, to signal the congregation's entry into sacred space. When we interviewed Charles, he told us that he had initially experimented with "smudging," the lighting of sage and the ritual invocation of the six directions using the smoke from the sage, a ceremony based upon rituals from some Native American tribes.

Charles found that the sage smoke was too heavy and some people reacted to it physically or emotionally. The copal provided a smell and scale of ritual that seemed more appropriate, so he abandoned the use of the sage. When we wrote up our interview later, we realized that we had missed an opportunity for deeper conversation. We had not questioned whether the use of the sage represented an inappropriate uprooting and transplanting of a Native American ritual for a service primarily attended by and built around white European cultural traditions. In a later conversation with Charles, we learned that he has participated in ceremonies performed by Native American leaders for many years and has received permission to lead some of these ceremonies on his own.

Many worship leaders, both clergy and laity, have been challenged by agitation and reflection from our fellow Unitarian Universalists regarding cultural misappropriation in worship. As more and more UUs experienced anti-racist and anti-oppression training during the eighties and nineties, the concept of *cultural racism* became more widely understood among us. In the 2001 article "Reckless Borrowing or Appropriate Cultural Sharing?" by Jacqui James, the late UU minister Marjorie Bowens-Wheatley has explained that the term *cultural misappropriation* is used to describe:

> consciously or unconsciously seeking to emulate con-
> cepts, beliefs or rituals that are foreign to a particular
> framework, individual or collective. It is incorporating
> language, cultural expressions, forms lifestyles, rituals or
> practices about which there is little basis for direct knowl-
> edge, experience or authenticity into one's being. It is also
> the superficial appreciation of a culture without regard to
> its deeper meaning.

Scholarly study of cultural misappropriation has looked at many diverse practices that go far beyond worship:

• The marketing of one culture's artifacts or symbols for economic gain, such as Polynesian-themed restaurants and mass-produced aboriginal art.

- The disrespectful borrowing of images and symbols from one cultural tradition for a very different context or activity, such as the use of the Native American names or images for sports teams.

These appropriations will be embedded in popular American culture as long as they have an economic payoff.

It isn't easy to determine who owns the expressions of a particular culture or who is entitled to give permission to use them. In a world of instant communication, rapid travel, and multicultural cities, how can we tell whether it is cultural misappropriation or cultural cross-fertilization when the arts of one culture are explored by those who belong to a different culture? After almost two decades of engagement with these issues by UU worship leaders, this conversation continues to widen, including more people and deeper engagement throughout our Association.

During the 1990s, conversation about cultural misappropriation in the UU tradition was limited to leaders who were actively seeking to apply their learnings from anti-racist, anti-oppression work to the development of curriculum and program materials for congregations. When the UU Women's Federation (UUWF) commissioned Elizabeth Fisher to write a new adult religious education program on feminist theology, the variety of voices and cultures from around the world that she drew upon to create that program challenged her to reflect on the difference between cultural appreciation and cultural misappropriation.

In 1995, the same year that the UUWF published Fisher's curriculum *Rise Up and Call Her Name*, Rev. Marjorie Bowens-Wheatley published "Cornrows, Kwanzaa and Confusion: The Dilemma of Cultural Racism and Misappropriation" in the *Journal of Liberal Religious Education*. Bowens-Wheatley brought to this article her experience as a member of the ministerial staff at Community Church of New York, a congregation well-known for including in its liturgical year worship services adapted from the religious holidays of the diverse cultures represented by its own members, such as the Jewish Days of Awe, the African-American Kwanzaa celebration, and the Hindu Divali celebration. Her article continues to stand out as a comprehensive and concise analysis of the issues involved in cultural misappropriation.

At the 2001 Unitarian Universalist Association General Assembly, the conversation expanded to a wider circle of UU congregational leaders than ever before. The spark for this expansion was the invitation to all the UUs attending this convention's opening ceremonies in Cleveland, Ohio, to join a march of witness protesting the Chief Wahoo logo outside the Cleveland Indians' baseball park, Jacobs Field. Wayne was active in organizing this protest, and as he studied the issues involved, we both appreciated in a new and deeper way how the insulting use of Native American images and symbols by sports teams is part of the same continuum of cultural misappropriation that includes a white minister in a UU congregation offering a smudging ceremony because he likes the symbolism and the smell.

It has been easier for UUs to appreciate the social and political insights of scholars writing about broad forms of cultural misappropriation than to apply this analysis to Sunday hymn and song selections or to rituals. While some uses of music can easily be understood as inappropriate when care is not taken to introduce and educate the congregation about the cultural context of the selection, other uses under challenge strike many church musicians as harmless. These musicians raise the concern that excessive worry about such issues will force them to sacrifice wonderful music and rituals from around the world. Those who argue against the claims of those concerned about cultural misappropriation point to the difficulty of defining a "culture," of identifying who owns it, and of describing how harm is created by sharing another culture's music.

Singing the Journey, a supplement to the UU hymnbook *Singing the Living Tradition*, was compiled and published in 2005 by a team of church musicians and clergy who were committed to making more resources from the world's musical traditions available for our services. Rev. Jason Shelton, director of music at First Unitarian Universalist Church of Nashville, contributed an essay entitled "A Perspective on Musical and Cultural Appropriation" to the interpretive materials accompanying *Singing the Journey*, and we commend it to all UU worship leaders. Shelton has influenced our best understanding about cultural misappropriation and the skillful means available to us for bringing cultural resources from around the world into our worship. Shelton writes,

> My experience has been that some people will start talking about "cultural appropriation" when what they really mean to say is that the musical offering or ritual just experienced was done poorly. Many Unitarian Universalists, it seems to me, are not comfortable making a judgment about the quality of a presentation, but are somehow OK with raising cultural or racial issues instead. I have been a part of numerous worship situations where the songleader has bounced and shimmied through a poorly sung African-American spiritual. Do I think that what they did was cultural appropriation? No—I have seen songleaders from many cultural traditions, including African-Americans, do the same thing (please do not assume that every African American can sing or lead spirituals well—stereotypes are very dangerous). I think what happened was that a person who was not really familiar with a particular musical style tried to lead a congregation in something that was beyond his or her particular musical skill. Such a situation is not only disrespectful to the musical tradition which has just been trampled upon, but also to the whole congregation, regardless of personal ethnic background, all of whom deserve better.

Transformational worship expands each participant's experience of their own boundaries, helping us to see that we are bigger than our own skin, our own neighborhood, our own culture. The conversation about cultural misappropriation raises a crucial question for the future of Unitarian Universalism: Who are "we"? When we use that pronoun, are we speaking only of UUs who come from European heritage? Are the cultures of the world without representation among our congregations' members? Of course not. Are the minority cultures represented in our congregations "not us"?

We believe that limiting Unitarian Universalist worship to elements that have roots in the Western European heritage of our congregations and of most of our members would be a tragic mistake, and that this is not the goal of our educators who call for increased cultural competency and sensitivity. The objective is to engage us all in an educational process that is vital for those who want to create culturally diverse worship models. It is a conversation we cannot afford to avoid simply because the questions involved are hard to discern and harder to answer.

There are several different ways in which cultural contexts for worship elements can be framed—in advance of a service, in the accompanying order of service, during a service, or after a service has concluded. Respect and engagement with other cultures on their own terms is a powerful teaching that is true to our Unitarian Universalist Principles. We can promote this lesson week after week through leadership and education around and within our worshiping community. The third section of this book has a chapter that goes deeper into concrete suggestions for respectful engagement with other cultures through worship while avoiding cultural misappropriation ("Honoring and Respecting Our World's Cultures").

Inviting and Including All Generations

The key, in our view, to developing enthusiasm for regular intergenerational worship services is this: Everything that makes your worship service more accessible to children makes the service more accessible to adults as well. Despite the stereotype of our congregations as being filled with sophisticated people with affection for the rational and the intellectual, there is still something of the childhood learner within each of us that makes us appreciate a well-paced service that makes its points clearly, briefly, and vividly.

During our sabbatical, the congregation we serve underwent a major building renovation that made our sanctuary unavailable for the entire fall. We also faced the loss of many classrooms that were routinely used for Sunday morning religious education. We had to make a decision about whether to rent space off-site to house religious education classes or find a way to keep families together in the limited space available in our building.

Director of Lifespan Faith Development Kathy Strawser and the sabbatical minister who took over during our absence, Tamara Lebak, met with us to consider options. Kathy and Tamara embraced necessity as the mother of invention, suggesting that we keep everyone together in the existing building, turn the available classrooms over to the pre-kindergarten children, and make the entire fall schedule of services intergenerational. It was all very intriguing and—for the two parish ministers, anyway—terrifying. But Tamara and Kathy would be the primary leaders for most of these services, and their vision was compelling.

Our congregation is like many others in the UUA, with a significant number of members who are seniors or single. We had a strong history of religious education ministry, which included both monthly children's services and a full intergenerational service every six weeks or so, often associated with holidays. More frequently, we had a story for all ages early in the service and then allowed the children to leave for their classes. A recent wave of babies among our members brought some tensions within the congregation, as new mothers who preferred to bring their children into the sanctuary with them struggled to make the right decision on when to take a restless child outside. Our fear about trying a full season of intergenerational services was that our faithful adult attendees would find such services boring. We knew that some of our members simply tolerated or skipped the Sundays with intergenerational worship, believing that there was nothing there for them. They grudgingly acknowledged that it was an obligation of the church to offer these kinds of services in order to recognize the presence and needs of the younger families among us.

As we talked about the possibility of a full fall season of intergenerational worship, Kathy and Tamara shared their vision of opportunities contained within these services, rather than obligations. When we came back from our sabbatical, we found a congregation that had been through a transformative experience we had not expected. They not only put up with the stresses and strains of crowded intergenerational worship in our social hall with good humor, but they repeatedly told us how much they enjoyed the creativity and content of services that were offered for all ages. We surveyed parents about their experience, asking whether they wanted to return to the previous model of occasional intergenerational services; they said no. They wanted to have their children in religious education classes during the services, but they also wanted monthly hour-long intergenerational worship services in the sanctuary to continue.

There seem to be two historically predominant models for involving children in worship so that they might begin to engage with worship as a lifetime spiritual practice. Each of them has its shortcomings. In one model, the experience of worship is introduced, and the skills learned, but in a setting isolated from parents and the church's larger worshipping community. When the children do come into the sanctuary, it's for an event that doesn't feel connected to the full worship experience. The main feature of this visit to the adult worship service is the story for all ages. Many of us have attended these occasions over the years, with a minister or religious educator offering a story to a crowd of children sitting on a carpet. Sometimes the story connects with the larger themes of the service; sometimes it doesn't. Children are shown pictures in books that the adults can't see, so many adults just watch the kids, who become a show in themselves. The story ends, the children are sung out, and everybody feels good about being an intergenerational church. The children may have absorbed a lesson from the story, but have they learned anything about worship? While the peer context for learning in this model of worship is important, but it lacks a sense of connection to the larger world of possibilities.

Some religious traditions fully immerse children in the

congregation's worship life. Church school classes and worship are for all ages and follow one another. Children sit with their parents through a full service directed primarily at adults. For many children this experience is boring and alienating. It can also be difficult for parents, especially those whose children are unhappy and restless. Some people have told us that over time, this kind of immersion in worship has had a happy outcome. This is especially true for children whose parents engage with them about the worship experience and bring them regularly to church. These children develop knowledge, understanding, and skills. They know the liturgy and have certain important sections of it committed to memory. They carry these experiences with them into adult life and are better prepared for a lifelong engagement with worship as a spiritual practice.

Neither of these models is adequate in and of itself. We have come to believe in a third model that supplements the first and is more accessible and satisfying than the second. It counts on parental involvement and engagement in a way that can work for diverse family structures. It's the exception rather than the rule to see families coming together to church consistently week after week. Single-parent and divorced-parent families are less consistent in their attendance. Parents struggle with having their children in church with them every Sunday but want them to experience a full service. Children need peer-group education with leaders and teachers, but they also need to be able to tell their parents what they are experiencing and feel like it connects with what the parents are doing.

Our model of intergenerational worship involves regular children's worship services as part of church school, plus monthly all-church intergenerational services for kindergarten age to grandparents, where families are encouraged to sit together and experience the whole service. Planning these kinds of services has taught us a great deal, not only about what is important for teaching the worship experience to children, but also what will create transformative worship for all ages. (See "Intergenerational Worship.")

We find at West Shore Church that the things we do well in intergenerational worship teach us new things about how to improve the other three services a month. Worship is not an adults-only activity. On the contrary, it engages that part of us that is forever young, forever opening our eyes in wonder and discovering the world as brand new.

Music for the Community

It was the first anniversary service of the September 11 terrorist attacks and the sanctuary was full. Like many of our colleagues, we felt the need to respond to the anniversary with a worship service. We gathered readings and consulted with our musician, who would play on the organ Barber's "Adagio for Strings," and, at the end, "God Bless America." Wayne had just heard Bruce Springsteen's latest release of a song called "My City of Ruins," and decided he wanted to play that song as part of the liturgy. Our music co-director was amenable to the suggestion, although his personal policy was not to play recorded music when a live musician was available. We put the service together and, with our congregation, participated in our rite of mourning and reclamation of hope.

Some time later, we heard feedback about the service from two individuals. One was a church member who loved the music of Bruce Springsteen. She said that when she heard the song's chorus, "Come on, rise up! Come on, rise up!" she started to weep, both because of the power of the words and Springsteen's voice, as well as hearing an artist that she admired and respected played in her own church. The other person expressed a sense of shock and dismay at hearing a contemporary artist played during such an emotionally charged service. This person thought the music was inappropriate for the occasion and wished we had maintained a certain standard of classical music throughout the entire service.

It might be tempting to believe that these two church members represented generational poles. However, the Springsteen lover was a sixty-something-year-old grandmother of two, who frequently attended rock concerts. The woman who preferred classical musical was in her twenties and sang in our church choir.

Regardless of congregation or denomination, opinions about the style of music featured on Sunday morning continue to be a challenge for church musicians and members alike. In many religious traditions, there is a body of musical works that are considered sacred—works that are composed for or are inspired by religious services. Johann Sebastian Bach signed many of his pieces "for the Glory of God alone," to state that his sacred music was written to tell the Christian story from a devotional perspective. One would not, for example, expect Bach to have played his "Coffee Cantata" during an Easter worship service. There was an appropriate time and place for secular music, but it was not in the service on Sunday morning.

Unitarian Universalists have not felt the same restrictions applied to their musical offerings. UU music directors have been free to choose from a vast array of musical selections, both sacred and secular. In our combined years of UU worship leadership, we have used everything from Bach's "St. Matthew's Passion" to the Grateful Dead's "Box of Rain"; from Bartok to George Gershwin; from Indian ragas to a choral arrangement of a piece from the musical *Rent*. Unitarian Universalist churches have long incorporated a variety of musical styles into their worship, most notably jazz and folk, without any controversy. However, the philosophy behind selecting anthems or other special music is different in a Unitarian Universalist setting. Our music may reflect the glory of God, but more often, it expresses the depth and breadth of the human experience. This considerably broadens the repertoire; if UUs believe that, as Peter Mayer's lyric states, "everything is holy now," then all music has the potential to be appropriate for worship. If all music could be appropriate, what standards do we apply in selecting music for a given Sunday?

All discussion of music has a subjective component. Although most may agree, for example, that the work of the great European baroque, classical, and romantic masters is "good" music, it won't appeal to everyone's taste. Although many agree that the music of John Coltrane is "good" jazz, some may feel it doesn't belong in church on a Sunday morning.

During our sabbatical we attended over two-dozen churches on Sunday morning and experienced almost every style of music available. We heard "high church," enabled by a budget that could afford the best organ, musicians, and singers from a major metropolitan city. We heard jazz combos and light country-rock bands. We attended worship services in a rented school auditorium and in a black box theatre, featuring local talent on electric instruments. We worshipped in megachurch stadiums with their own in-house rock bands.

Our experience of the quality and value of these styles depended on the skill and enthusiasm of the musicians and how the music fit into the service. Music becomes transformative when the musicians are dedicated to excellence and when the lyrics or the quality of the music itself take us out of ourselves for a period of time. That doesn't mean that music should be chosen to manipulate the emotions of the congregation. Rather, the music can point to an abiding presence—a deeper witness—a more profound sense of the holy. The questions to ask when choosing music include: Does it have the power to express the ineffable? Can it be done with excellence?

Most Unitarian Universalist churches prefer to hire someone who has at least one degree in music and/or can play classical music. This level of musicianship is the norm for Unitarian Universalist churches that can afford to hire a music director. Church members expect concerts outside of Sunday morning to be a regular offering of their music director. Choirs take on challenging music and offer it either on a special music Sunday or at additional concerts for the larger community. This standard of excellence has long been the hallmark of music and musicianship in Unitarian Universalist churches. It is a heritage of which we can be rightfully proud. Unitarian Universalist churches can boast of having some of the finest choirs, organists, and music programs in their cities.

Still, there is Bruce Springsteen. There is the music of U2 and the Dixie Chicks. Some Unitarian Universalist musicians write music in a popular genre, expressing the ineffable using twenty-first century instrumentation. There are now many styles of world music that music directors can choose to include in their repertoires. Unitarian Universalists must wrestle with the questions of whether any style of music can support the theme of the worship service, and whether musical variety means watering down the standard of choral, solo, and ensemble musicianship that UU churches have worked so hard to establish.

Ministers want to take advantage of any resources for a worship experience that will add to the meaning they hope to convey. Ministers also vary in their level of musical education and in their understanding of the issues involved in selecting music. Music directors frequently hope that by choosing music that is more challenging for the common ear they will elevate their listeners. Laity may be divided between those who appreciate more complex pieces and those who feel left out and frustrated. Choir members may be excited by the high standards of choral selections chosen by their music director, while longing to perform a popular song from a current musical.

These diverse needs and interests can come together. It is possible to maintain Unitarian Universalist traditions of classical European compositions *and* bring in the fresh sounds of jazz, blues, country, gospel, folk, alternative, and rock and roll, without compromising the integrity of the worship experience. We believe that expanding our repertoire to include music from all the continents and all styles of music is a theological imperative for Unitarian Universalists living in a post-modern culture. (See "Hymns and Music.")

While on sabbatical, we had a regular opportunity to sing hymns from the pews instead of from the pulpit. At one particular Unitarian Universalist church, Kathleen recalls standing to sing and then feeling that something had gone terribly wrong. Was she singing off key? Too loudly? She soon realized that the problem was neither of those possibilities; it was that her voice stood out like a flute solo because no one was singing around her.

Although the hymn was musically excellent, the congregation did not know it very well. When the upper notes went beyond an E-flat, people began to drop out. The tempo was too quick for a first-timer. There was no identified song leader, so most people were left to struggle to find the melody line on their own. Furthermore, the dissonance between the organist's flourishes, and the uncertainty about the tune compelled our fellow worshippers to abandon hope and simply mouth the words or pray for the whole hymn singing experience to end.

Should hymn singing be a challenge or a comfort? In her article "The Music in Churches Project: The Views from the Pews," published in *Congregation* (Alban Institute, 1992) Linda Clark writes of her experience trying to sing a new hymn:

> That was a completely new one for me. Yes, that was the one that had two different versions, the single line and the harmony one. And I got mixed up halfway through the second verse. I kept saying, "Which one am I supposed to sing?" And that was a distraction to me, interestingly enough, although I do remember singing it, and enjoying it and liking it. But then being distracted when I thought I was going down and somebody else was going up. I thought, Oh, I don't care! I'll just do it my way!

Clark's experience gives us a clue to the success of what is called Christian praise music. We attended several churches that used only praise music. There were no bound hymnals, no organ accompaniment, and no complex hymn tunes. The words were projected on a screen; the tune was simple and repeatable; and the accompaniment was usually by a band composed of guitar, bass, drums, and keyboard. The projected lyrics allowed the congregation to participate fully, and the experience was very user-friendly.

This approach does not bode well for the future of hymnody. Trained musicians may look at praise music with some mixture of pity and even contempt. It does not challenge singers to stretch their musical vocabularies. It is often simplistic and not regarded as intellectually astute or theologically profound. It caters to the reality that musical education is becoming increasingly absent in public education, thereby making it difficult for people to know how to sing or even what good singing might sound like. Unitarian Universalist musicians have worried that the adopting praise music will make our worship services less rich in history, tradition, and musical nuance.

One alternative to the praise-music phenomenon is to take some of our cherished older hymns and recast them in a new musical setting. At an emergent church in Colorado, we found hymns that were a mix of new praise-style music and standard hymns set to a rock and roll beat. We were surprised to discover how much we enjoyed singing the traditional "All Creatures of the Earth and Sky" as a praise tune—underscored by a rhythmic beat and a lead guitar. The text was simultaneously projected on the screen, alongside pictures of Saint Francis of Assisi, some contemporary renderings, and photos of the stained glass windows of Gothic cathedrals. By chance, the Unitarian Universalist church we attended the following Sunday used the same hymn, but our experience was much different. We sang it from a hymnal, accompanied by a piano. The tempo was dreadfully slow. Instead of being swept up into the music, we slogged through the hymn and were glad when we finished.

A second alternative is to write music that can be easily sung—a Unitarian Universalist version of praise music. We found the best example of this at a congregation in Texas, where Rev. Christine Tata wrote songs with meaningful yet simple lyrics. An opening praise-type hymn invited us to enter into holy time before the call to worship. Set to a rock beat, with words projected on the screen, "Holy Time" allowed both of us to participate despite our different levels of musical ability. More important, we quickly felt we could sing this hymn by heart, and we remembered it long after the service was over.

Singing the Journey: A Supplement to Singing the Living Tradition (2005) was designed to expand the variety of hymns and songs easily available to UU congregations. In the foreword, Rev. William Sinkford writes:

> My hope is that our congregations will find in this book music that will shape our community and give new voice to our values as we move forward, supporting our deepening faith and a more effective voice for justice. And I trust that we will come to love these hymns, and in time, to sing them passionately without looking at this book.

The hope then, as expressed by Sinkford, is that Unitarian Universalists will develop a repertoire of hymns that are known by heart, much as our grandparents could sing "I Come to the Garden Alone" or "The Old Rugged Cross." Many of the hymns in the supplement may eventually work their way into the minds, hearts, and liturgies of our UU congregations. Some of them, such as "Where Do We Come From?" or "Building Bridges" are short enough to memorize and the tunes are easy to sing. Others, such as "Blue Boat Home," are quickly becoming favorites, although unlikely to be learned and sung by heart. We would like to see a hymnal supplement of praise music for Unitarian Universalists—accessible music that can eventually be learned and sung from memory. These hymns would be written in layers. That is, the melody line would be discernable to the untrained ear and easy to sing. For the musically trained singer, harmonies could easily be added. For the musically trained instrumentalist, additional descants and accompaniments would be written. Woven together, these musically literate and theologically meaningful tunes could be sung by all, regardless of musical ability. This style of hymnody is the wave of the future.

Thinking about the future of Unitarian Universalist hymnody, we question whether the era of publishing a new hymnal every twenty years or so has passed. We recognize that bound hymnals provide a historical document of our denomination's theological and musical journey. They are something tangible that can be found in Unitarian Universalist churches all over the country. Sharing a hymnal with a stranger or a fellow church member is an act of intimacy that projected words simply cannot foster. At the same time, hymnals are expensive to produce, purchase, and maintain. They cannot be adapted so they become closed canons. They are not created to allow words or tunes to be projected on a wall.

While we're not willing to give up on bound hymnals yet, we do suggest exploring other possibilities for the future of our hymnody. Perhaps the next hymnal would be a loose-leaf binder that allowed hymns to be removed or added as the need arose. We hope for a widely used website, where church music could be downloaded for a fee and legally copied for congregational use. Additional orchestration and augmentation of hymns could be purchased through the site by church musicians. The download could be formatted to be projected on a wall or a screen. While this kind of availability of fresh music resources is routine in evangelical traditions, we have only just begun to explore the future of UU hymnody.

Announcements as a Bridge

The first Unitarian Universalist church Kathleen attended was a small congregation in Northeast Ohio. That congregation had a curious ritual about announcements. At some point in the general din of loud conversation that occurred before the service, a man with a large voice would walk around the church foyer and half sing/half-shout: "announcements, announcements, annow-ow-nce-ments"! The purpose of this was to get us all to shut up, sit down, and listen to the news of the church and all the opportunities for involvement that we should not let slip by. Announcements are ubiquitous in our services of worship. Of the congregations responding to the 2004 survey taken by the Commission on Appraisal, 92 percent reported that announcements were made during services, making them the most widely shared component of UU worship. Despite their popularity, announcements are often the bane of worship leaders. It seems that everyone who tries to come up with a good strategy for the length, control, and placement of announcements struggles with different opinions about what to do with them.

We believe that the issue is not what should we do with announcements, but rather how they fit into the reasons we gather for worship. Our response to the question of whether and how we have announcements in our services reveals much about our theology of worship, how we feel about the flow and drama of the service, and where authority in a congregation is vested.

Congregations whose history, culture, and theological majority call for a worship service that is understood as praising God might have a stronger tendency to eliminate announcements or segment them either before or after the actual service of worship. The majority of Unitarian Universalist congregations, however, lean more towards the common denominator definition: that worship is "holding up things of worth and value." Their announcements are strategically integrated into the service, because they reflect the congregation's sense of what is worthwhile.

The argument for the value of announcements to the church community is easy enough to make. Announcements are one way the community speaks to, for, and about itself. They frequently extend invitations to participate in the congregation's ministries, service opportunities in the larger community, or events that reflect core values of the congregation. They serve an important administrative and public relations function in our contemporary culture, where information overload can mean that many worship attendees have skimmed or ignored the monthly church newsletter.

When announcements are done well, they can point to the church's overall vision and mission. Does the church offer opportunities for spiritual deepening and practice? The announcements should reflect this mission. Does the church see itself as a place to care for the wounded and weary? The announcements will embody that ethos. Does the church see itself as a community that invites both direct and systemic justice-making service to the wider community and to the world? The announcements will point towards that concern. Too often, the announcements reveal that the church sees itself as a club for its members, with entrance available only to those who can interpret and filter the announcements.

A lot of energy can be devoted to deciding where to put announcements. Placing them at the beginning gets them out of the way. To accommodate latecomers, they can go midway through the service. At the end of the service, they can be a kind of commissioning before people leave. The unavoidable problem is that by their very nature, announcements are inevitably for the people already in the pews. Rarely will newcomers take away more than a broad first impression of the priorities of church life from verbal announcements. Increasingly, congregations in other traditions that emphasize Sunday morning as a guest-friendly time minimize or eliminate announcements during the service. Those that are made are closely tied to the primary mission and identity of the church and usually point to an opportunity for follow-up to the message or theme of the service.

If you decide to have announcements, you will always be trying to strike a balance between nurturing the existing community and making guests feel welcome and included. Keeping that balance in mind, here are some things to consider:

Be clear where the authority for making decisions about announcements lies. Our smallest family-sized congregations, with fifty people or fewer in worship, and with many lay-led or guest minister services, usually have authority diffused among the members. Any volunteer in charge of any area of church life is invited to or feels entitled to access to the announcements. In larger minister-led congregations, tensions around how announcements are controlled can reflect balance-of-authority issues among the professional leader, the staff, the governing board, and/or the worship committee.

Ministers might choose to do the announcements themselves because they feel they can offer them more efficiently and succinctly, or because it sends a message about who has oversight of the church's programs and activities. A minister might ask a member of the governing board to routinely offer the announcements. The church's tradition might be that board members always do the announcements because that represents to them the lay authority in the congregation having a voice in the worship service. If the minister never offers announcements, does that mean these institutional and community concerns are beneath the attention of the minister? Does it simply mean that this is a convenient place to add a lay voice into the service in a segment where there are not high expectations for a professional standard of presentation? A surprising amount of subtle meaning can be contained in the choice about who offers the announcements.

Often the by-laws of a church that describe the authority of a minister are forgotten or ignored when it comes to deciding who offers the announcements. If the by-laws or the congregation's traditional practice make it clear that the minister is given full authority for the creative management of the congregation's worship life, that should include the decision about how or even whether to have announcements. The larger a congregation is, the more clearly that authority will be understood. Larger congregations are more likely to either minimize or eliminate announcements at the minister's request. If announcements are retained, it is more likely that the large church minister will see them as a component of worship that deserves time, attention, editing, and thoughtful placement that reflects the congregation's culture and theology. UU congregations of all sizes, however, increasingly are making the choice to delegate oversight of all announcements to the minister, because they value their being done smoothly and professionally, within modest time limits.

The boards of smaller lay-led congregations need to understand that the best practice for empowering lay leadership is to avoid inserting themselves into areas of congregational life where they have delegated authority. The announcements should not be seen as a board-owned piece of the worship service that stands apart from the authority of the committee charged with preparing worship.

Consider a formal or informal "announcements policy" that is consistently applied. Ministers or lay worship leaders who have the authority to regulate announcements are well advised to consult either formal or informal networks of authority in the congregation's culture to help them determine the policy. Whether that policy is formally written down, decided by some authority group, or published in the church newsletter would depend on the culture of the church and the intensity of feeling around announcements. Our experience is that the people in the congregation who are most focused on the details of a policy are those who are most invested in stretching it for their own use. Most people have singular or occasional requests for verbal announcements and are content to abide by a policy that they believe to be fair and impartial, if they are confident that there are other ways their message can be heard.

A minister's or trained lay leader's delivery of announcements is usually more smooth and well timed than those made from the floor. Ministers and lay worship leaders should devote writing and even rehearsal time to ensure that announcements are as clear and crisp as fifteen-second commercials, which is about the attention span any of us have for absorbing their content anyway. Worship associates programs might start with training on announcements before moving into readings, prayers and meditations, and sermons.

Make only announcements that pertain to the entire community, and prioritize announcements based on whether they provide opportunities for follow-up to the message or theme of the day or involve events and opportunities that are closest to the core mission of the church. As a last priority, allow announcements that have some institutional urgency due to short-term deadlines.

If you have both Joys and Concerns and Announcements, separate them in time in the order of service, and speak promptly and directly to people who seek to abuse the Joys and Concerns section of the service with disguised announcements.

The placement of announcements can vary greatly and still be appropriately integrated into the flow of the worship experience. We have seen announcements done well before the prelude, after the benediction, as a component of the second portion of a service involving concerns of the community, and as a bridge to the offering that precedes the readings and sermon. We have also seen them done badly at all these points.

Announcements may seem like a simple matter, until and unless they become a focus for conflict. That's when it's important to understand the underlying issues, and how your congregation has missed having an open conversation about them.

Worshipers recognize when the components of worship have been carefully constructed to reflect the themes of the day and the central mission, vision, and values of the congregation. They may not all be able to articulate how the planning and structure of the announcements helped make that connection, but they will leave the service better prepared to embrace the opportunities for service that the worship experience has offered them. And to guests, announcements can sometimes say more about what a congregation truly worships than anything else in the service.

Encouraging Generosity

During one month during the early 1980s, Wayne had an opportunity to attend a Unitarian Universalist service in a larger urban congregation and to preach in a small congregation in a college town. The two worship services had many things in common, despite the fact that these congregations were different sizes and served very different memberships. He was particularly struck, however, by one important difference—how they conducted an offering.

In the larger congregation, with its older traditional sanctuary, its rows of pews, and its team of ushers, the offering was listed in the order of service. It was announced with thoughtful words by the minister and accompanied by one of the organ pieces featured for the day's service. At the end of the collection, the ushers processed down the aisle so that the minister could offer a blessing over what had been received that day.

In the smaller congregation, with its informal, multipurpose worship space in the former living room of the house they owned, there was no usher team and no offering listed in the order of service. Instead, the lay leader briefly drew attention to the fact that the congregation was supported by pledges and gifts and reminded people that there was an offering basket in the hallway. On the way out, Wayne found a wicker breadbasket balanced on the edge of a radiator, with no signage indicating its purpose.

Our ministry careers have encompassed service to UU congregations of all sizes in four decades, and we have seen (to use Charles Dickens's phrase) "the best of times and the worst of times" for the offering as an element of our worship. Each of these two UU congregations had come to their approach out of their own history, culture, and theology. In that sense, each approach had some integrity for their context of worship.

The congregation that minimized the offering words and simply left out an inconspicuous basket gave Wayne the feeling that they thought it was inappropriate to talk about money in church. When he asked one of the members about this at coffee hour, he was told that the big evangelical Christian churches on television were always pushing for more funds—something that was not acceptable in a UU church.

When it comes to deciding how to conduct an offering in worship, a deeper question must be asked: How can we encourage the practice of generosity and an attitude of abundance in Unitarian Universalist congregations? The offering is the opportunity we have to respond to that question in worship each and every week.

The familiar Biblical quotation from Timothy 6:10 reads: "For the love of money is the root of all evil." We have attended UU congregations where that seems to be a predominant belief, at least in terms of how an offering is acknowledged and handled. The congregation described above made the offering an afterthought, but there are also UU congregations that continue to avoid any offering whatsoever on Sunday mornings. Some congregations seek to distract worshipers from the fact that an offering is happening by minimizing the invitation to give and maximizing the offertory music.

In many congregations people pass the plate or basket very quickly, as if the contents carried the bubonic plague. Those that contribute do so surreptitiously, carefully covering the currency with a full hand so that it is not visible to their neighbors. When the collection is over, it is rushed out of the room as if it were a bomb. A sigh of relief from the ushers responsible for its counting and safekeeping tells us that this disagreeable task is over for another week.

All of these behaviors are understandable in the context of attitudes towards religious institutions and money that are prevalent in liberal churches:

- The liberal church raises the money it needs through a rational moral appeal, rather than through an emotional appeal.

- The liberal church plans its budget annually and supports it through pledges, making the weekly offering a convenience for delivery of pledges rather than a weekly necessity to pay the bills.

- Liberal churches aren't focused on money, but on education, programs, and services.

- Money is private. It is impolite in our churches to get too focused on or pushy about money.

- We're different from the money-grubbing fundamentalist TV churches that exploit their members and viewers financially to enrich the lives of their entrepreneurial ministers.

Whatever you think about the accuracy of these descriptions, and whether you recognize them in your church, it is worth considering whether your congregation uses the offering to reflect a very different set of attitudes about money. Rather than the love of money being a root of evil, the attitudes we see reflected in some worship offerings ask us instead to consider our relationship to money as an expression of our love:

- Our relationship to money is an expression of what we value and how we can harmonize our actions with our beliefs.

- Our relationship to money is experienced rationally, emotionally, and spiritually. The church is a place where all of those dimensions can be experienced and openly acknowledged.

- Generosity is a spiritual practice that should be invited as a part of church life. Like any spiritual practice, generosity involves regular disciplines and commitments of time, and a certain measure of sacrifice of other competing values.

- The church need not insist on being the highest priority for members' generosity, but it needs to remind its members that there is no one else but us who can ensure the survival of Unitarian Universalist institutions and values in coming generations.

- Generosity is a source of joyful living and creates abundance.

The offering is not a necessary evil intruding into the service; it is part of the liturgy. We have been encouraging everyone at our services to contribute as an act of liturgical participation. Whether they are people who pledge and pay their pledges outside of Sunday morning, whether they are nonmember attendees, whether the offering is for the work of the church or for an outside agency or cause, we encourage everyone to join in.

In this respect, we treat the offering as we do the hymns or responsive readings. A worship experience that uses hymns, litanies, or responsive readings is much more satisfying if most of the people present engage with the experience. You feel a little uneasy if you are the only person in your row singing along with the worship leader. If everyone in your section ignores the invitation to join in a responsive reading, wouldn't you ask yourself if there were some disdain for this element of worship, a sort of liturgical civil disobedience? What then, do our members, our friends, our visitors, and our children feel when an offering is announced and requested, and the majority of those present ignore the request? We experience embarrassment. We ask ourselves whether a person checking out Unitarian Universalism for the first time draws the conclusion that this is a stingy congregation, or that they don't trust the integrity of the worship leader's request.

We believe that all the elements of a worship service are important and reflect opportunities for spiritual growth and engagement in daily life. The value of generosity is well established and supported in our tradition and as a hallmark of religious living in the world's religions. The offering is the time in each service when the value of generosity is held up and encouraged and acted upon by making a contribution that is as much symbolic as it is effective.

In saying this, we don't mean to denigrate the concrete value of the money being contributed—it is an important component of church budgets or church philanthropy toward needs in the community. Regardless of the amount that is collected in the offering, and regardless of whether that money supports the operating budget of the church or a justice-seeking activity outside the church, the act of contributing something is important to each person attending. It is a way of representing and acting on the value of generosity, and affirming the possibilities for abundance in our common life.

During our travels we experienced several satisfying ways of making the offering a transformative moment:

An Ordinary of Offering. In this context, *ordinary* describes elements that are repeated each week. The words that introduce the offering have been developed by many congregations into a recurring element of worship that people know by heart, inviting them into a familiar and important practice in their service.

A "Stable" of Offering Rituals. Alternatively, some congregations prefer to develop a "stable" or series of offering introductions with which the congregation becomes familiar. These words can be used from week to week to create a combination of familiarity and variety in the way the offering is invoked and invited.

Testimonial Opportunities. We came across one congregation that routinely had members offering brief testimonials about how the practice of generosity had come alive for them through their participation in the life of the church.

Appropriate Offertory Music. There's a balance to be struck between overwhelming or disguising the liturgical act of giving and minimizing the value of the musical offering. Music in itself is a gift that is given to all of us during a worship service, whether it is offered by volunteers or professional staff. The offertory music usually does not demand full attention from the congregation (such as a choral piece) since there are distractions and requirements involved in the ushers moving about to receive the offering. It should nevertheless be strong enough to pull the attention of the worshipers back to the piece after they have finished engaging with the offering ritual.

Closing Ritual. Most often this ritual involves an usher or usher team bringing the offering forward so that the gifts given can be acknowledged and consecrated. Although this latter word is not popularly used by many Unitarian Universalists, it simply means that the acts of generosity involved in this liturgical ritual have resulted in financial resources that are made "sacred" by our intentions. Closing rituals require some training and even rehearsal for the ushers participating in them. An alternative can simply include another ordinary element in the service, a short prayer of thanks and blessing indicating that the offering has been received and that we are grateful for it.

One further question is how to use the offering. The latest trend, at least in larger UU churches, has been to give it away. Although special collections or the practice of a monthly social-action offering have long been a staple in Unitarian Universalist services, twenty-first century UU congregational consultants such as Michael Durall and Dan Hotchkiss have encouraged churches to give away the offering every week, and many of them have listened.

The consequences of giving away the offering have been consistent from congregation to congregation: The amounts collected increased, often dramatically. Congregations that double and triple their Sunday collections are not uncommon. The impact on the operating budget usually can be absorbed, since the unpledged income brought in by the offering plate is rarely significant. Congregations that want to try this approach sometimes begin by implementing a monthly social-action offering for a designated cause, and discover that they can sustain the income line item in their operating budgets and increase their generosity in the community or denomination many times over. Books and articles such as Durall's *Creating Congregations of Generous People* (Alban, 1999) and *Beyond the Collection Plate* (Abington, 2003) or Hotchkiss's *Ministry and Money* (Alban, 2002) are excellent resources for delving deeper into why this practice works. Our purpose in this book, however, is to consider the offering as an element of worship. We think that the practice of giving the offering away increases generosity because it is one more way that worshipers can look at their worship attendance as an opportunity for participatory spiritual practice.

In earlier days, church members who were regular worship attendees brought their weekly or monthly pledged offerings in envelopes to be put in the plate when it came around. In the congregation we serve, this option is still possible. However, more and more of our members use electronic checks, credit cards, and checking account debits to make their pledge payments. When the offering plate comes around, they let it go by because they have not been encouraged to understand a different meaning for the offertory as an element of worship. Regular giving away of the offering makes it a reflection of the mission of the church to feed the hungry, to create justice, and to engage in partnership with institutions outside the church that share those goals. It is a reminder that our worship is not simply for ourselves, but transforms us into people who can make a difference in the world

Increasingly, in some Unitarian Universalist intergenerational worship services and in children's worship, parents are encouraged to help their children participate. Rather than looking at such encouragement as involving lessons for children, we remind our congregation that we are encouraging the liturgical practice of generosity and abundance from an early age because it expresses and reinforces these values for all of us. We encourage everyone to see the offering as a worshipful act, not a pragmatic necessity.

The message in so many religious traditions about money is that the world makes an abundance of resources available to us if we generously share what we have. Jesus' parable of the talents, the story of a rich master who gives his servants significant sums of money to hold while he is away, is a good illustration of this kind of stewardship. Two of his servants invest the money and make a profit for him. The third is afraid he might lose it, so he buries the money and returns it intact, but not multiplied. The message from the master to the third servant is that to him who has more, more shall be given.

We've always looked at this parable not as an endorsement of free-market capitalism, but rather as a message about faith in abundance as a component of stewardship. The talents are the sums of money given by the master; to us they represent the resources we have available in the life of the church. Each of us receives these talents in different proportions, and each of us has a spiritual responsibility to use them for the good of everyone. When we are able to do that, we will see a return in abundance of resources that goes far beyond anything we would have realized if we had kept our talents buried. Just as many congregations are discovering that giving the offering away paradoxically results in more money being available for church generosity, encouraging everyone to make small gifts each week as part of the liturgical life of the congregation will help create a culture of abundance in congregational life that will benefit the health of the community for many years to come.

Sharing Joys and Concerns

A congregation we once belonged to had developed a very meaningful liturgical ritual for sharing joys and concerns. After the sermon, an invitation was extended for those who had a joy or concern to share to come forward, light a candle on the altar, and speak briefly into the microphone.

Over time, the congregation had developed a good understanding about this element of the service. When it was used for political announcements or lengthy speeches about personal issues, the offenders would usually get gentle feedback from friends in the congregation, rather than a chastisement from the minister. Most Sundays, the joys and concerns were meaningful and appropriate.

All of us would get a little nervous, however, when one particular member came forward. Betty (not her real name) was a long-time member with a history of mental illness. Our relationship with Betty had taught us to be more inclusive and comfortable with people with mental and emotional disabilities. Over time, we learned about situations and conversations that made Betty uncomfortable, and she learned about appropriate boundaries to observe in her interactions with others—until one Sunday when she decided to take part in Joys and Concerns.

Betty began with "Dear God"—and had no sense of when to stop. Finally, the minister had to gently interrupt and thank her for the way she had shared. The following Sunday, Betty was up first when the invitation to Joys and Concerns was extended. This time, she was able to figure out when to stop.

When the third Sunday in a row came along, the minister realized that there was something going on beyond Betty enjoying the act of prayer and the attention it brought to her. During the week, Betty had called the church office four times to respond to newsletter announcements that were framed as invitations. Several of them were things that she had no interest in, but she felt obligated to respond anyway.

It turned out that politely responding to formal invitations was a social skill Betty had been working on through her therapy. Her decision to respond to the invitation to express joys and concerns on that first Sunday was based on the belief that this was something she was supposed to do as a good church member, just as she was supposed to respond by phone to all the invitations in the newsletter.

When the minister talked to Betty, he told her that the invitation didn't mean she had to personally respond every week; once a month might be a better schedule so that everybody who had a joy or concern got a chance. Betty appreciated the guidance, and "Dear God ..." was heard regularly but not weekly thereafter. Lately we've heard that when Betty feels moved to speak, her prayerful reflections pick up on some underlying theme within the service, like a jazz musician improvising off the main melody.

Betty's story illustrates some of the joys, as well as some of the concerns, about the liturgical ritual our congregations call Joys and Concerns or Joys and Sorrows. In more traditional Christian worship, there is often some form of congregational prayer or prayer response, which allows worshipers to call for or offer names or circumstances for which congregational prayer is requested. As this form of prayer became less desirable for the more humanist-oriented Unitarian and Universalist congregations in the decades immediately preceding and following the merger, nothing rose to take its place.

Like the ritual of chalice lighting, the origins of the Joys and Concerns ritual is difficult to trace. The element of lighting a flame or candle is present in both. Our memories and our review of orders of service from the 1960s and 1970s suggest that congregations were looking for ways to bring more symbols and rituals into their services during those decades. "Candles of Concern" is one form that emerged from this search. Seen from the perspective of Christian worship practices, Candles of Concern combined the Catholic practice of lighting devotional candles honoring a loved one with the practice of inviting prayer out loud from members of the congregation on behalf of a person or a difficult life situation.

In smaller congregations where sermon talkbacks were routine, it wasn't much of a leap to include a time for presermon "talk-before" in the form of a time for joys and concerns, with or without candles. As with many other worship innovations in our movement, the practice spread through ministers seeing this innovation offered by their colleagues, either in seminary or in congregations they visited, or through lay leaders attending a service at a general assembly or district meeting.

The positives associated with sharing a time of joys and concerns in worship are many:

- The opportunity for people to speak in their own voices about their own lives invites an engagement with the worship experience unlike any other.

- Members of the congregation come to know one another better.

- Pastoral concerns are held up, and follow-up occurs not only through the formal ministries of the church, but informally, simply because people know and care about a concern that has been expressed.

- News within the congregation that has not made its way into the written order of service or newsletter can be shared without the need to run it past a minister or staff.

- Visitors to the congregation get the feeling that this is an open, warm, and caring congregation as they hear members sharing difficult life issues or wonderful milestones.

- The life issues expressed remind us every week that joy and woe are woven throughout our lives, and that religious living involves engagement with the whole of life in community.

- The ritual of coming forward and lighting candles or speaking into the mike creates an opportunity for movement, and a change of pace and voices, that makes the flow of the service more interesting.

With all of these positive benefits that can be associated with a time of joys and concerns in worship, why have many UU congregations, particularly the larger ones, moved away from this ritual? Some of the reasons have to do with what works well for congregations of different sizes. Many larger congregations, especially those with an historic order of worship to which they were committed, never tried incorporating a joys and concerns ritual. Those that did found that some of their expectations about what this ritual would bring were not met.

In larger congregations, people often have different expectations about the relationship between the individual and the collective in worship. They don't expect to know or be able to respond to the concerns of every person in the church community. While they anticipate that their pastoral concerns will be heard and answered, they assume that this will happen through contact made with the ministers or trained volunteers, and not informally through an announcement of need in a worship service. In these congregations, the setting for worship is usually more intimidating for people uncomfortable with public speaking. The invitation to speak about one's life through a microphone is more attractive to extroverts, and extremely hard to resist for people with boundary issues who enjoy an audience, so open-invitation rituals can routinely be dominated by a small number of voices. It reminds us of the way that many Internet chat groups start off as a wide-ranging conversation among many diverse people, but eventually settle into a pattern where a handful of people dominate the posts.

This balance between recognizing individual concerns and honoring collective concerns (as well as an overall concern about worship quality) has driven many of our large congregations away from an open-microphone style of Joys and Concerns. The lead minister carries responsibility for all that happens in the worship services. The minister is extremely conscious of the visitors at the service and the fact that worship is the most important first impression for any newcomer. The unpredictability of an open microphone Joys and Concerns can affect the message, timing, and emotional content of the service for visitors and regular attendees alike. The most common compromise position for larger congregations involves rituals of concern, such as candle lighting, combined with an opportunity to express in writing a joy or concern that the writer would like held up in public or private prayer. The minister or worship leader may then incorporate that request in the pastoral prayer during the service.

While this ritual may work better in congregations with fewer than 150 people in worship, even these congregations need to be aware of how it can affect the feel and the meaning of the worship service, and consciously address those concerns in its design:

- Joys and Concerns will inevitably feel in-house to new visitors. The names, stories, and unstated assumptions about what everyone knows will make some visitors feel left out.

- It's hard to make Joys and Concerns flow briskly, as people come forward in sequence from their seats, speak, and return. Those unfamiliar with the microphone can have difficulty being heard. Sometimes Joys and Concerns feels like an interruption in the service flow rather than an integrated part of the service.

- There is always the risk of boundaries being breached, leading to disclosing confidential information, too much detail being shared, or time limits being exceeded to the detriment of the rest of the service.

- The line between announcements and the sharing of personal joys and concerns can be hard to draw and harder to enforce among strong personalities.

- A particularly difficult concern may be immediately followed by a light and celebratory joy that will be hard to honor as the impact of the previously expressed concern still resonates.

Each congregation will decide whether, how, and when Joys and Concerns is an appropriate element for their worship service from the context of their own history and worship culture. Any Joys and

Concerns ritual should be understood from the same perspective that ministers bring to their sermons when they contemplate including stories from their own lives. The purpose of such story is to talk about an individual's experience in a way that the emotions and events described become transpersonal. Everyone in the congregation should feel some connection, even if the experience is one they have never had, because the way the joy or concern is expressed is clear, brief, and universal. This is what a worship leader who receives joys and concerns on written cards with the intention of including them in a prayer is required to do. Congregations that invite open-ended joys and concerns should not be afraid to state expectations for how that segment of the service will be understood and used, including suggestions for format and length.

In reflecting on Joys and Concerns as an element of transformative worship, the first thing to acknowledge is that this ritual cannot be seen as more important than any other aspect of the worship experience. Its place and weight in the overall service must be considered in the context of all the other possible elements of worship. How the ritual feels to newcomers as well as to regular attendees must also be considered. Finally, the tension between the symbolic role that the ritual plays in the service versus its functional importance as part of the pastoral ministry of the congregation should be explored and clarified.

The design of the ritual can offer a response to all of these considerations, allowing both the guest and the long-time member to feel that this congregation cares about its members lives and wants the worship service to reflect the range of human experience and emotion that is present in the service every week.

Prayer and Meditation

Across all sectarian and faith boundaries, all over the world, prayer is the most common element of worship. Times of prayer or meditation in Unitarian Universalist worship can have a powerful impact on our religious community. Setting aside this time in weekly worship is not just a nod toward tradition or appeasement of the more spiritually oriented types. Praying together as a religious community—whether that means sitting together in silence or being led by the leader in a time of prayer—acknowledges that our lives are not entirely our own, that we are creatures in an interdependent web. Prayer can give voice to the often unexpressed longings of church members. Prayer can name out loud the compelling issues of our time and fashion a vision of the world made fair and all her people one.

If the time devoted to prayer, meditation, and contemplation lies at the heart of transformative worship, then it is important to explore the ends to which this time is directed. The acronym ACTS reminds us of the four categories of traditional prayer—Adoration, Confession, Thanksgiving, and Supplication—and provides a useful place for us to begin to understand the transformative possibilities for prayer in Unitarian Universalist worship.

Adoration is not a word that most Unitarian Universalists are comfortable with. Traditional adoration language from the Bible includes naming God as Lord, Master, King, Prince, Exalted One, Heavenly Father, etc. Most theistically inclined Unitarian Universalists are uncomfortable with such patriarchal and hierarchical language. Probably our favorite expression of adoration is simply Spirit of Life, taken from the well-known and much beloved hymn composed by Carolyn McDade. The term *Spirit of Life* appeals to both the theist and the nontheist. It acknowledges the larger reality of life in which we exist, while acknowledging there is another dimension to life that we don't all see or comprehend in the same way.

Under the title "The Image of God," Kathleen's former homiletics professor created this table of prayer:

Adjectives	*Nouns*
Eternal	God
Loving	Spirit
Demanding	Love
Healing	Mother
Unknown	Father
Intimate	Jesus
Challenging	Presence

The point behind this prayer exercise was to pair up a variety of adjectives and nouns and see how they felt. "Eternal God" is fairly standard, but what if one prayed "Eternal Mother?" Or, for example, if one coupled "Challenging" with "Love," what might the rest of the prayer be like? Unitarian Universalists are uniquely poised to experiment with the question of to whom prayer is addressed, for we acknowledge that life's greatest mysteries cannot be named, although we continue to attempt to find names for them.

Confession is a practice not often found in our churches. Unitarian Universalists have long rejected the notion of original sin, so the idea of confessing our sins publicly or through the act of prayer seems outdated. For some who grew up in churches where confession was a regular practice, being free of it is a relief. There is generally only one time during our liturgical church year that Unitarian Universalists will engage with a liturgical act of confession—the Jewish High Holy Days, including Yom Kippur. The one confessional responsive reading found in *Singing the Living Tradition* was written by Rob Eller-Isaacs, and is often used during the Sunday acknowledging Yom Kippur.

It is our belief that it's time for Unitarian Universalists to reclaim the act of confession. Confessing does not make one inherently bad; it simply means acknowledging that we, too, are part of the brokenness of the world and that it is our responsibility to be in right relationship with self, others, and the larger world. Being in right relationship means that we make amends when necessary, and we ask for forgiveness or we offer forgiveness when it is asked for. To confess as part of our prayer life is a humbling experience that provides a necessary counterbalance to our often heady insistence on our inherent worth and dignity. Confession is a spiritual discipline and should be incorporated into our private and public prayer life.

Thanksgiving is probably the easiest prayer for Unitarian Universalists to both write and speak aloud. We are an appreciative people, thankful for our health, our lives, our communities, for liberal religion, for one another. We give thanks for food, for our ministers, for our volunteers, for our programs. The traditional act of thanksgiving—giving thanks for both joys and sorrows, but most of all, for a people's relationship with the Divine—is well represented in scriptural texts such as the Psalms.

Supplication is defined as the act of making a humble, earnest petition. Unitarian Universalists are often also uncomfortable with this traditional category of prayer because it raises deeper theological questions, such as: If we pray for something that doesn't happen, does that mean our prayer was ineffectual? What if we don't believe in an omnipotent God with the power to grant our requests? And what about trivial supplications, such as "God, please let our team win this game?" Unitarian Universalists are rightly uncomfortable with this kind of supplication. We don't believe in a God who is a substitute Santa Claus, dispensing favors like toys from a large knapsack. Nor do we believe in a vengeful, punishing God who withholds love or doles out sorrow in retribution for our sins. Instead, the best understanding Unitarian Universalists may have of the purpose of supplication in prayer is embodied in Abraham Heschel's words, found in the hymnal *Singing the Living Tradition*. Heschel writes: "Prayer invites God to be present in our spirits and in our lives. Prayer cannot bring water to parched land, nor mend a broken bridge, or rebuild a ruined city, but prayer can water an arid soul, mend a broken heart and rebuild a weakened will." In our own tradition, Rev. Lon Ray Call expressed the same thought more briefly: "Prayer doesn't change things—prayer changes people and people change things."

When we ask for something through prayer, whether it be as global as world peace or as specific as a release from personal suffering, we must understand that the miracle of prayer is not necessarily in the granting of a wish. It is in the act of praying itself—asking for what we need, stating our vulnerabilities—that the magic and mystery of prayer occurs. To make a prayer of supplication is to take a stand for hope and, regardless of the outcome, hope ultimately sustains us all.

Some Unitarian Universalist congregations avoid using the word *prayer* entirely and list in the order of service something less fraught with theological baggage. They may use the words *meditation* or *reflection* to describe a time of interior seeing that takes the form of an interlude of silence, perhaps introduced by spoken words. The

English word *meditation* comes from the Latin *meditatio*, which means contemplation. Meditation in many traditions is the practice of clearing the mind from distractions and focusing on the simple reality of what is. Often, a single point of focus, whether a word, a mantra, or simply counting our inhalations and exhalations, is the entry into the spiritual practice of meditation.

What then, is the difference between prayer and meditation as elements of transformative Unitarian Universalist worship? Theologically, the difference might best be described in the words of author Edgar Cayce: "Through prayer we speak to God. In meditation, God speaks to us." In practical terms, the difference between a prayer and a meditation in Unitarian Universalist worship seems to rest on whether the worship leader addresses the Mystery of the Universe and then uses a traditional form of prayer, or begins with no formal address and instead describes a person, scene, object or circumstance to use as a meditative focus. Without giving these distinctions much thought, many congregations and ministers use the word *meditation* to describe a quiet reflective part of the service which can be focused on either images or aspirations. Some congregations take this one step further to include guided meditations, with explicit direction as to the images or thoughts that guide worshipers during this time.

It's been our experience that meditation often gets short shrift because of the pressures involved in a sixty-minute worship service. To engage more deeply with meditation as a spiritual practice takes a minimum of ten minutes to still one's mind, with the following ten minutes the most focused part of the contemplation. Most worship services cannot afford to spend that amount of time in meditation, so we often allow a minute or so—a pause, really—for meditation, reflection, or prayer. That time is not wasted; for many in the pews, those few moments are the only time in a week they will take to be still and silent. Even more important, it is a time to be silent together, which is a different experience from being silent while driving alone or taking a solitary walk through a park.

While any element of the service can become a gateway to an engaged religious life, this is especially true of prayer or meditation.

The question for us as worship leaders is how to invite and engage people whose experience of prayer or meditation in worship has made them want to explore these practices more deeply. We encourage our ministers and religious educators to look for ways to include contemplative practice opportunities in the life of the church. No matter who leads these practices or whether they are seasonal or weekly, contemplation, meditation, and prayer should never be isolated within worship. Rather, they should act as an invitation to a personal practice that will deepen any Unitarian Universalist's religious life, regardless of theological identity.

The Liturgical Year

In published works available to all congregations or within their own congregations, some Unitarian Universalist ministers have tried to define our liturgical year, often following a calendar of themes influenced by religious holidays, both sacred and secularized. What is missing from these attempts is any shared sense that we have a single common story to tell. The closest we come to claiming that story is in the ways we talk about the history of the free church and its connection to our traditions. A few of our churches have attempted to use historical figures and occasions as the milestones of a liturgical year, but the practice has not spread.

Lectionary preaching in support of a commonly accepted liturgical year is therefore not widely practiced among Unitarian Universalists, with the exception of a small number of our Christian UU ministers. We have also avoided lectionary-based worship because of two great liberating innovations. The first is the freedom to draw upon all the scriptural traditions of the world's faiths as a source for the readings that companion our sermons. When Unitarians and Universalists gradually let go of their exclusive Christian identities in the first half of the twentieth century, the movement in that direction was inaugurated by ministers who introduced readings and sermons based on texts outside the Christian tradition. The second liberating innovation is closely related. Those ministers who introduced non-

Christian scriptures to their liturgies and preaching also drew their readings from secular sources, from the "scriptures of humanity." Inspirational poetry and prose that might have previously been quoted in a sermon began to appear in the honored place previously assigned to the reading from scripture. As this transition moved gradually from innovation to standard practice, lectionary preaching among UU ministers gradually faded away.

Lectionary preaching became a lost art in Unitarian Universalism because it was associated with an authority structure that we no longer could honor. Despite the fact that it is associated with a Christian approach to creating liturgy, we have reflected a great deal about the possible value to our congregations of the disciplines of the liturgical year and the lectionary. Transformative worship has to be firmly planted in time, yet reach out beyond time. Without a common story that frames our church year, we need to be conscious of the progress of our liturgical year, anchoring our services in time.

Since 2004, All Souls Church in Tulsa has been developing a lectionary approach to monthly themes for their services and educational programs. This approach is lectionary in the sense that they are working on publication of a three-year calendar that reflects a monthly curriculum of great theological themes and spiritual questions for those seeking to live a liberal religious life. An increasing number of UU congregations have been inspired by All Souls or by similar practices in evangelical churches that tie these themes into small-group ministry conversations, religious education classes, and adult programs.

Congregations and ministers that have not developed this idea quite so fully nevertheless routinely use certain lectionary practices as they decide on their sermon themes. The typical liturgical year of celebrations and religious holidays honored in contemporary Unitarian Universalist churches begins with the Ingathering Sunday often associated with Water Communion. The Jewish Days of Awe, which include Yom Kippur, follow the lunar calendar and occur anywhere from early September to early October. During the 1950s and 1960s, United Nations Sunday was a routine part of our liturgical calendar, but this practice has faded along with our hopes for the UN's ability to prevent war. The pagan rituals of Samhain or the Mexican celebration of the Day of the Dead influence the ways we now incorporate Halloween and its accompanying Christian holidays of All Souls' Day and All Saints' Day. Thanksgiving and Christmas round out the calendar, with December being a complex month for worship, including the possibility of themes associated with Buddha's Enlightenment Day, world AIDS day, human rights, winter solstice, and Hanukkah.

In midwinter, Martin Luther King Sunday is widely celebrated in our congregations, and Valentine's Day offers many ministers an occasion to preach about relationships. The spring equinox provides a fixed celebration, but the date of Easter varies, and the two can be combined in worship, depending on how close in time they fall. Earth Day is increasingly a mandatory service theme, especially in churches working towards a Green Sanctuary designation. Two-thirds of our congregations have a spring canvass, so an annual Stewardship Sunday will be held sometime in the early spring. The older tradition of Children's Sunday is represented by a variety of springtime services that close out the church school year: Coming-of-Age services, Youth Sundays, and intergenerational services all have their places in different congregations. Flower Communion, the ritual originated in Prague by Unitarian minister and martyr Norbert Capek, is celebrated anywhere from Easter to mid-June as a component of spring-themed worship services or as a stand-alone service, often focused on international Unitarian Universalism. Many congregations also include special annual Sundays and worship rituals, such as membership ceremonies and child dedications, that have emerged from their own particular history.

This narrative of a typical church year would probably accurately describe the milestones in the liturgical year that are celebrated in 90 percent of our congregations. It reaffirms the fact that despite our avoidance of the Christian story, we are nevertheless attracted to an informal liturgical year that provides a structure for sermon ideas, whether or not there are monthly liturgical themes. When monthly themes are chosen, however, there is even more direction offered for the liturgy and the preaching. Few ministers using monthly themes feel bound to offer three or four sermons a month on that theme, choosing instead to highlight it strongly once or twice each month, and incorporating it on other Sundays through liturgy rather than through the sermon.

We encourage lay worship teams, worship associates programs, and our colleagues in ministry to plan for worship four to six months in advance, with their congregation's liturgical year in mind. We also encourage exploration of the monthly thematic approach to service planning as a routine component of the lay theological education that is part of congregational life.

One of the congregations we visited, First United Methodist in Fort Worth, Texas, offered a contemporary service that used a liturgical year format inspired by the work of Matthew Fox, president of the Institute of Creation Spirituality in Oakland, California. Fox has proposed a five-season liturgical year based on broad themes:

- *Via Positiva* (summer; themes of in-gathering and celebration)

- *Via Negativa* (fall; themes of contemplation, silence, making room for the mystery)

- *Interlude for Festival Time* (from Thanksgiving to Christmas)

- *Via Creativa* (winter; themes of bringing something to birth in the midst of winter)

- *Via Transformativa* (spring; themes of Easter, resurrection, the transformative power of life, sending forth, transformation by the word)

We think that Matthew Fox's work suggests creative possibilities for Unitarian Universalists to rethink their liturgical year and a lectionary of potential themes.

The Sermon

Our work in this book is about the linkages that make a transformational worship service an integrated whole. Much of the UU writing about sermons has considered the art of preaching in isolation from the other liturgical elements of the service. In this section, we want to explore the linkage between the readings and the sermon, and consider how the sermon is linked to everything else in the service.

As inheritors of the Calvinist Protestant emphasis on the spoken word as the central sacrament of worship, we have always accepted that preaching holds the key to how a worship service will be experienced. Nevertheless, we believe that the meaning to be found in a transformational worship experience stems from the care and creativity that shapes every element of the service, not just the sermon. Insofar as the sermon is in harmony with other elements of the service, they illuminate each other. The other elements must also be able to stand on their own in conveying meanings, especially when the sermon falls flat.

The most satisfying worship experiences we had on our sabbatical were ones where the sermon wove together many of the images, texts, and stories we had experienced in the other elements of the liturgy. We particularly noticed the absence of this interrelatedness when we felt that the hymns and particularly the readings had been chosen primarily to fill slots. Choices like these usually paid some attention to the time of the year or the theme of the sermon, but it was obvious that the sermon preparation had not been powerfully informed by the readings.

Even though lectionary preaching may be a fading art among Unitarian Universalist ministers, we have noticed in interviews with our colleagues a new interest in sermon preparation rooted in a textual exegesis. One of the most exciting conversations we had during our sabbatical was with Rev. Dr. Mark Belletini, senior minister of the First Unitarian Church in Columbus, Ohio, about the spiritual process of sermon preparation based on texts. Belletini told us: "The way that I view the creation of worship as art form is to be an exegete of the readings—to weave the readings in and throughout the service and sermon. Sometimes I'll take two readings and use one as the theme and the other reading as motif, but they all must weave together as a whole."

Members in Columbus told us that they sometimes found themselves drawn into Mark's sermon by their curiosity about how the readings he had chosen would tie together with the announced theme for the day and with each other. The readings are guides for the sermon, so they are chosen early. Mark lives with them for awhile before it is time to respond to them with the sermon. Because the readings are spiritually important to the whole service, Mark takes great care in selecting them. The two readings must always be from a man and a woman, and he strongly believes in identifying the readings by source and date. If he can't find the source or date of a reading, he will probably will not choose it. He also adds quotations at the top of the order of service, again from both genders.

We found ourselves remembering Mark's approach when we interviewed Rev. Dr. Laurel Hallman, senior minister at the First Unitarian Church of Dallas. Laurel also told us that for her the search for readings was primary. When she found the right readings, she knew what she would say in the sermon. She said: "What's important and different about UU preaching is that our text is metaphorical, and usually the best way to express ourselves through the text is through poetry, or an image…that's the way we do our best teaching… through image and metaphor…." Her curriculum "Living By Heart" invites an engagement with readings as spiritual companions that are a focus for the meditative disciplines of silence, memorization, and contemplation. Having lived with this discipline since first hearing about it from the late Rev. Harry Schofield, we were not surprised that Laurel promoted readings as preliminary to and primary for sermon preparation.

The attraction to using texts as informative tools arises from an increasing comfort among our ministers in preaching that is rooted in stories and images, as well as in intellectual theses. We have no doubt that many if not most of our UU church members will continue to say they enjoy our services for the "intellectual stimulation" they provide. Intellectual integrity and clarity will continue to be important standards by which our preaching must be judged. But worship that is transformative encourages preaching that also touches the heart and the imagination. When that happens, our worship experiences can truly become sacramental.

At the second UU Minister's Association Convocation held in 1980 in Newport, Rhode Island, Rev. Roy Phillips offered a reflection on sermons in which he described them as sacramental. Phillips described sacraments as liturgical elements and rites that are metaphorical. They point beyond themselves to something that the sermon text cannot embody or describe, but somehow assists the hearer in realizing. Just as the wine and bread in Catholic communion help the faithful to feel an intimate connection with their savior, so the sermon offers this same possibility for a transformative liturgical experience.

Phillips told a story about an "unspoken" sermon. One Sunday morning, a person in the receiving line asked for a copy of the text for that day's sermon. On the following Sunday, this person came back to Roy with a disappointed look. It was not the sermon the parishioner had asked for. Roy assured the person that this was indeed the text that had been preached last week, but the parishioner was unconvinced. The sermon preached was not necessarily the one that was heard, and the sermon that was heard was the transformative one. That's why even technically inadequate preachers can play meaningful roles in their parishioners' lives through their sermons.

When we asked a worship class of our church members to describe what can be transformative about sermons, we were impressed with the clarity and promptness of their responses. Sermons that help create transformative worship, they told us, have to be authentic, i.e., feel to the listener that they are coming from a real place inside the experience and understanding of the preacher. They have to tell the story of our tradition and our church, by pointing the way to the best we aspire to in our church community. One person told us that the best sermons take away fear. Asked to say more, she elucidated: "Fear of doubt, fear of ignorance, fear of failure, fear of loss."

Midge Skwire, minister emerita at West Shore Church, had the final word for our class: "I've always said that great sermons are deep calling unto deep." We love that phrase from the Psalms. Insofar as the readings and the sermon reflect that sacramental possibility—the deep in the author of the reading calling out to the deep in the author of the sermon—that dynamic will be reflected as well in the way members of the congregation hear the sermon.

Sending Forth

"Our worship has now ended. Let our service begin!" Variations on this theme are found in orders of service and in benedictions in many worship services. We like this way of thinking about the end of a service. It reminds us that our services do not exist for their own sake, but point beyond themselves to our life in the world, to how that life has been changed by worship and in turn can change the world. We also like the circularity of the service's conclusion, bringing us back to the world from which we came and sending us forth into it.

Endings and beginnings are not only intrinsically related. They are one thing. An ending can be a starting point in worship planning. We think about this when we decide whether the closing words should arise from the meanings found in this particular service, or whether they should be words used frequently in this congregation and well known to everyone. We think about this when we insert the words "Extinguishing the Chalice" into the order of service, and decide whether it will be extinguished with accompanying words. We also think about this when we decide whether the service will begin and end with music, and whether people are invited to bring their attention not only to the prelude but also to the postlude, remaining seated and listening to the end. Different congregations end their services with different degrees of attention to these distinct elements. There is no one right way to end a service, but there is a way that pays attention to how things end, what the ending means, and how the ending is actually a new beginning.

Our favorite metaphor for a service of worship is that of a hero's journey, and in this context the classic lines from T.S. Eliot remind us of where we want to be when the postlude music sounds. In *Four Quartets* he says that we will never stop exploring and the end of it all "will be to arrive where we started and know the place for the first time."

The literal translation of the Latin roots of the English word *benediction* is "speaking well." In the Roman Catholic mass, the benediction is a closing blessing from the priest upon the people. In the free church, we look to each other for our blessings, rather than to the individual authority of the minister as a mediator of the divine. Our two most recent UU hymnals have titled the section of closing readings "Benedictions and Closing Words," with no explanation about whether the editors saw these as two distinct forms, or whether they were simply using both titles to avoid complaints from local church members about an excess or lack of traditional religious language in headings. We like the word *benediction* and would argue that our UU benedictions have taken two distinct forms: blessings and closing words. These forms represent two distinct ideas about their relationship to the rest of the liturgy.

The benediction as blessing generally uses prayer forms or scripture quotes to send people forth with words that speak of our hopes for the lives we live and for the world that awaits us. Some classic scriptural words of benediction from the Bible are from Numbers 6, the blessing the Lord gave to Moses: "The Lord bless thee and keep thee, The Lord make his face shine upon thee, and be gracious unto thee, The Lord lift up his countenance upon thee and give thee peace."

This type of benediction need not have any thematic relationship to the rest of the service. Indeed, when a benediction as blessing stands alone it can be a unique element for the end of that particular service, or it can be an element that the congregation uses over and over. Many of the benedictions in our hymnals take the form of blessings. They use the prayer forms with verbs of invocation, intercession, and hope: "May we …" or "Let us …."

A benediction as blessing need not be in a prayer form or use traditional religious language, however. It is important that it calls out to a power that is larger than any of us alone and invokes that power to make real the hopes we share for our individual and common lives. One of our favorite examples is from Robert Mabry Doss, in *Singing the Living Tradition*:

> For all who see God, may God go with you.
> For all who embrace life, may life return your affection.
> For all who seek a right path, may the path be found,
> And the courage to take it, step by step.

The benediction as closing words generally relies on quotes from poetry or prose, or original writing from UU ministers. It is intended to reflect and wrap up the themes of the day's worship, and to send people forth to act on them in the world. Such benedictions are not in prayer forms, although they may have some of the rhythm of spoken prayer. A good example is an excerpt from Mary Oliver's poem, "In Blackwater Woods," found in *Singing the Living Tradition*.

These kinds of benedictions sound more like commissions. They remind the congregation to use the wisdom or strength they have found in worship to go back into the world and do what needs to be done. They can be chosen to echo a theme of the service, or even an author or reading source used earlier in the service. They can "arrive where we started and know the end for the first time" by picking up phrases or words from the covenant or bond of union that the congregation spoke near the beginning of the service.

The Hindu tradition offers us the word *mantra*, which helps us understand another function of the benediction in transformative worship. A mantra is a word, phrase, or scripture text (often containing a name of God) that is repeated over and over as an aid to meditation and a form of prayer. Many of our congregations have found that benedictions can be an important repetitive touchstone in the service, an element that is used in the same way each and every Sunday, and that the congregation comes to know by heart. We have noted earlier the value of considering repetitive elements in the service, as a means of having the congregation own their service, become familiar with it, and absorb certain components of it "into" their skin and bones and heart and head, speaking to them not only when they are in worship, but also when they are not. We have been struck by the number of UUs who carry with them a phrase or text, often a benediction, that they know from memory and repeat to themselves, both when they are in worship and when they are not.

Benedictions are particularly powerful elements to consider for such a role because they stand alone, like covenants or chalice lightings. They usually follow music, so their words stand out uniquely, and they are the last words that people carry out with them. They are words that speak to important elements of our living tradition and remind us of the power and comfort of our religious community.

During one of his ministries, Wayne routinely used a benediction that he had come to love, and he found members of his congregation asking for it to be included as the closing words at weddings and memorial services. Many people had committed it to memory and quietly recited it with him at the end of every service. Sometimes, benedictions such as this are strongly associated with one particular minister or era in the life of a congregation. New ministers can usually tell whether an element of worship they might want to change has truly been incorporated into the life of the congregation by the feedback they get.

Benedictions offer us the possibility to distill a truth in a succinct and poetic way that can encapsulate the message of a service or the meaning of the church community. They are live words that carry a lot of power, touching a deep chord in people's hearts each time they are heard.

In 1986, Wayne wrote the following benediction for a service at Thomas Jefferson Memorial Church in Charlottesville:

> Take courage, friends.
> The way is often hard, the path is never clear,
> And the stakes are very high.

Take courage, for deep down there is another truth.
You are not alone.

It was used in only the one service. Some years later he was asked by Helen Pickett if she could include this text in a book of worship materials she was editing entitled *Rejoice Together* (now in second edition, Skinner House, 2006). Helen published the benediction in her book, and this led to this benediction being included in the hymnal *Singing the Living Tradition.*

We have both been struck by how widely used this text has been, both as a spoken and a sung benediction. We think it's a good example of a worship element that works because it reflects both the invocation of a reality and power beyond ourselves and the fact that we look to each other for our blessing.

PRACTICAL DETAILS

Motivated ministers, worship committees, and worship associates programs try to improve the quality of their services by following checklists offered in dozens of workshops, books, and manuals. Sometimes these dos and don'ts are helpful. Other times, the resulting worship experience remains awkward and lackluster.

Transformative worship is not ultimately the result of good technique, but of a well-defined understanding of the church's mission and purpose, and a plan for the worship services to reflect that mission and purpose every Sunday. Each congregation or worshipping community must know what it is worshipping and why. When that purpose is clearly understood and stated, the worship experience has a palpable power, energy, and meaning.

Quality worship is also a cumulative spiritual practice. Its power in an individual's life is not understood through a singular service but through incorporating worship into a weekly discipline.

With a powerful purpose and a community of committed participants, the next steps toward transformative worship lie in the details: the planning and careful execution of every aspect of the worship experience, from the processional to the moment the worshipers head home.

The first two sections of this book were devoted to the "why" and "what" as opposed to the "how." This section reflects on the details, including tips on the practical "how-to's" of worship. If you are a lay leader or worship committee chair in search of some brief tips on creating better worship by next Sunday, each of these chapters has a bullet-point summary of best practices, either imbedded at the end of the discussion of a particular topic, or as a summary at the end of the chapter.

Processionals

Done well, processionals announce that we are making distinct entrance into holy or contemplative time. Not all Unitarian Universalist churches have a worship space that lends itself to a lengthy and dignified processional, but even if your congregation meets in a gymnasium or a storefront or in the round, you can still begin your service with the same effect as if you were processing down a long center aisle in liturgical garments swinging an incense censure.

At the Pathways Church near Dallas, in a service with forty people attending, we experienced a ritual that assumed the role of a processional, but was more appropriate for the rented school space they were using at that time. This opening ritual was created by the lay worship team. In the front of their worship space was a table prepared as if to receive guests. Atop the table were an attractive tablecloth, a centerpiece, and placemats. Stationed around the corners of the room were four church members, each holding a plate. At the appointed time, they slowly walked towards the table, holding their plates aloft. When they reached the table, they silently held up their plates before carefully placing them on the table, backing away, and taking their seats. The effect was that a place had been laid for the member and guest alike. Their silent, dignified, and intentional processional set the tone for the service. Without saying a word, their actions said, "You are welcome here."

Effective processionals are often rehearsed or, at the very least, thoughtfully planned. The first consideration is the choice of music. Does it have a "walking" rhythm? Funereal hymns or prelude music do not make for a processional that creates a sense of movement and excitement in the liturgy. If a band is used, does it inspire the participants to stand and move with the music or does it invite a passive performance-style response?

Who is in the processional? What are their roles? Where do they stand after entering the space? How fast do they walk? What is their body posture? How do they handle any objects they are carrying, such as candles, chalices, or banners? All these details make for a cohesive look and add to the drama of the processional.

TIPS

- Give yourself time to prepare for worship. Are you testing microphones five minutes before the service? Has there been musical rehearsal? Do all the service participants know how they will enter into sacred space?

- Be intentional about the beginning of the worship service. If there is gathering music of some kind, distinguish it from the prelude by a bell sound, a call to worship, or some other signal.

- If you have a choir that does process, make sure that they are clear about how to line up, enter, exit and where to stand. If there is no choir, the worship leaders can enter the space in a processional style, even if they come in from a side door.

- Those who process should walk with dignity—heads held high, hymnals up, shoulders back—and look as if they are enjoying the processional.

- Banners or flags or something vertical to carry add drama. One of the highlights of most annual district and general assemblies is the banner parade, which is a ritualized processional.

- Consider what people wear as they process. Is there a look or mood that you as the worship leader are trying to create? Do you want to evoke a sense of the holy, or a comfort with the casual? If a choir doesn't have robes, should people wear similar colors, or is that aspect not important?

Invocations

To invoke, from the Latin *invocare*, means "to call or to ask." The task of the worship leader is calling out to the continuity of Sabbaths and inviting the spirit of thousands of Sabbaths to join us for this particular gathering. "Good morning" is more suitable for a little talk in front of a breakfast club than as the words that begin worship on Sunday morning.

Worship leaders often make the mistake of confusing an invocation with a reading. Lengthy invocations that include the issues of the day, or the ninety-nine names of the divinity so as not to offend anyone, are a sure way to put your congregation to sleep right off the top. Remind the congregation that they are co-participants in a great drama that involves theological reflection, social action, pastoral care, education, and service. Keep it simple, brief, and powerful. Invoke the spirit of whatever you hold dear—but for God's sake—invoke something!

TIPS

- Go directly into your opening words, invocation, or call to worship. Avoid introducing them or identifying the author. The author is usually noted in the order of service; if not, read the words and then say: "the words of _____."

- Don't choose or write an opening that is too lengthy or dense. Six to eight lines is about right, unless it's an unusually compelling piece of poetry or prose.

- Invoke the spirit of whatever you value the most, whether that is God, the Spirit of Life, the highest values in human nature, or something else.

- Find ways to be creative with the invocation. Can you sing it? Can you speak it and then sign it? Can the choir, a soloist, or a cantor do it on occasion?

Covenants

Some readers will immediately identify the covenantal components of the worship service in the church they attend or lead. Perhaps they are explicitly identified in the service or recited or read in unison every week. Perhaps the covenant is the reading that accompanies the lighting of the chalice. Perhaps the covenant is the congregation's mission statement that appears in the order of service every week. Other readers will ask themselves whether their worship includes a covenantal practice.

Most congregations already using covenantal affirmations in worship have arrived at their covenant via one of two paths. They have drawn upon historic covenants that survived because they succinctly and poetically sum up important meanings and promises. When no historic covenant exists, they have engaged in small group or congregational reflection processes around creating a unique covenant that speaks to the promises made by this particular congregation's members. Such an undertaking must be well conceived, and there are resources available from the UUA or neighboring congregations that can help.

If your congregation has no obvious covenantal element in worship, and if you are a layperson intrigued by the possibilities for a covenant in your service, talk about it with your minister. Be clear where the authority and responsibility for worship planning and leadership in the congregation lie. If you are in a lay-led congregation, see what you can find out about the history of liturgical elements in the service. Start with understanding what has happened in the past as a means to discern what would engage the congregation in the future. We were pleased to come across the original "Bond of Union" created by the charter members of West Shore Church in 1946, which had not been well known or used for many years. We brought it back as one element of a new membership ceremony in our services.

If the traditions or attitudes in your congregation suggest that recitation of a covenant in worship every week would be difficult, you can think about incorporating covenants as occasional ceremonial elements in services that recognize leadership or ministries that the congregation wishes to celebrate. Since covenants are promises, it is particularly appropriate to include them in ceremonies recognizing transitions in board or ministerial leadership, ceremonies that commission worship teams or pastoral ministry teams, or ceremonies that welcome new members.

Some congregations have created covenants that make explicit their standards for how members engage with each other in their spiritual searches, and also how they engage in disagreement, conflict, and political controversy within the church community. Such covenants are particularly important to hold up and celebrate in worship.

All these opportunities for affirming covenants remind the congregation of the power and importance of this central movement of the heart for people of a free religious faith. Worship is transformational for people's whole lives, not just for singular encounters with the mystery of life. It is transformational through the repeated engagement with promises and practices that build a deep connection with a tradition and a community of faith.

TIPS

- If your congregation does not use a liturgical covenant, discuss with the minister the introduction of a covenant into the worship life of the church. This is not something that should be done without careful thought and consultation.

- Examine your church's history to see if there has been in the past something that was used in the liturgy that may be helpful in creating a covenant for today.

- If your congregation already speaks a covenant, encourage the congregation to learn it by heart. A memorized covenant can have power and meaning in the lives of congregants both inside the church and outside its walls, as a readily accessible summation of the church's mission and meaning.

- Consider the different places or occasions in worship that covenants can be used. Don't limit yourself to thinking only about one part of the service, such as the chalice lighting.

- Consider using covenants for special services and rites of passage.

Lighting the Chalice

With the proliferation of chalice lightings has come many artistic and technical variations on the practice. One of our favorite stories is about a congregation that had a permanently displayed chalice designed with a gas jet available to create the flame. A control in the pulpit allowed the minister to flare the flame whenever desired; the temptation to create special effects emphasizing sermon points was almost too much to resist. The impulse to make the lighting of the chalice into a highly dramatic element of worship is well intentioned but usually misplaced. It can distract from the quiet power that the symbol offers as a point of entry into sacred space.

In examining this element of worship, consider the size of the chalice and its location. Think about whether it will be visible to all attending the service, how they will view it from a seated position, and whether they can see the flame over the edge of the chalice bowl. We cannot count the number of times we lit chalices and noticed too late that the flame was too small or low to be visible to the congregation.

One question that often arises is whether to use a candle or a lamp for the flame. Each has their advantages and disadvantages. Candles are reliable in the size of the flame they produce and the duration of their burning, except when influenced by HVAC drafts or window breezes. Oil lamps and fuels should be carefully matched with wicks that are an appropriate size to prevent the flame from smoking. Denatured alcohol is an attractive alternative to lamp oil, producing a clean-burning flame that can be controlled by the height of the wick. It has to be re-filled weekly because it evaporates quickly, and it should be lit ten minutes in advance of the service to burn off alcohol vapors.

Give thought to the placement of the chalice lighting in the order of service. It is almost always in the initial section of the liturgy, marking entry into sacred space and time, and holding up important values or the covenant of the congregation to all present, especially visitors.

If there are multiple service leaders, it is wise to assign the roles of chalice lighter and reader in advance to avoid confusion. Chalices are lit from the side, not from the front. Timing the lighting to a point in the accompanying reading adds dramatic effect, for example, to a place where words match the act ("We light this chalice to affirm …") or where a value needs to emphasized ("Love is the spirit of this church"). If there is a child involved, consider the height of both the chalice and the child, and whether the child can actually ignite the wick without a boost. (See "The Power of Symbols" for a description of a chalice-lighting program.)

In a simpler order of service, the lighting can be the one point where a dramatic action involving a unifying symbol of our identity is engaged. It behooves us to approach this action with care, clarity, and dignity. While some congregations effectively use the chalice lighting as a symbol of an honored role in the service for a lay speaker, we encourage you to let the power of the symbol and the ritual speak for itself, accompanied only by beautiful and simple words of covenant or inspiration.

Leaving the chalice burning at the end of the service is a liturgical mistake, in our view. The service has both a beginning and an ending as a sacred drama and exists in a different time from the world. Extinguishing the chalice at the end of the service should not be an afterthought; the chalice that is publicly lit should be publicly extinguished. Sadly, there is only one reading in *Singing the Living Tradition* for the extinguishing of the chalice—written by Elizabeth Selle Jones—which may explain the short shrift this action receives in our liturgies. It is, however, one of the better summaries of the chalice symbol and what it means to Unitarian Universalists of all ages:

We extinguish this flame, but not the light of truth,
the warmth of community,
or the fire of commitment.
These we carry in our hearts until we are together again.

TIPS

• Decide on the best size and design of the chalice for your congregation, given the worship space.

• Experiment with a candle, lamp oil, and denatured alcohol. Strive for that which gives the cleanest burn and emits the least amount of smoke.

• Invest in proper lamp or candle lighting utensils, and a candle snuffer.

• Have everyone who lights the chalice practice doing it at least once before the service, paying attention to body position and sight lines.

• Extinguish the chalice with the same care and dignity with which you lit it.

Hymns and Music

Unitarian Universalists pride themselves on their theological diversity. We enjoy the fact that an atheist, a pagan, a Christian, a Buddhist and a plain vanilla Unitarian Universalist can all sit together in the same pew, worship from the same hymnal, and celebrate both their diverse and their common theologies. Shouldn't the music that is played for prelude, offertory, postlude, and anthem reflect diversity as well?

Musically diverse congregations actively seek to expand their knowledge and respect for the cultures of the world by using different kinds of music in their worship service on Sunday mornings. They would employ the sounds of the Native American flute, the Indian sitar, the drums of Africa, and the chants of monks in Tibet, always with context and background provided so that these artifacts are not appropriated without reference to their culture and tradition. They might delve into the archives of ancient traditions and discover Gregorian chants or teach Appalachian shape note singing. No instrument should be excluded from worship—including the banjo, the singing saw, the penny whistle, or the electric guitar. This is part of what it means to live in a postmodern culture—that the musical instruments of the eighteenth, nineteenth, and early twentieth centuries are no longer the only ones available to us in the planning of our twenty-first-century worship experience.

There is no longer a central, agreed-upon standard of music for Unitarian Universalist churches. In the first half of the twentieth century, there was likely little or no discussion about the kind of music that should be played on the piano or organ, or sung by the choir. Choirs and church musicians drew on the standards of music from the baroque era to the twentieth century, with an emphasis on classical and romantic composers. As jazz and rock and roll emerged, they were definitely in the secular camp and were not considered appropriate for church music programs. Folk was the radical departure of choice for musically innovative UU churches. Today congregations of all sizes are drawing on all kids of music.

In the twenty-first century we see more and more musicians from popular culture whose message is spiritual, but not considered Christian rock. Bands and songwriters like Coldplay, Indigo Girls, Ben Harper, Nine Inch Nails, Jewel, Joan Osborn, and U2 all have songs and lyrics that are theologically articulate and sound. The challenge of engaging with popular music is how to weave it into a worship service. Do you play the CD? Can you get a choral arrangement of "I Still Haven't Found What I'm Looking for" by U2? And if you could, would it have the power and import of Bono's singing? What about hiring a band for Sunday morning worship? Do they play covers or should they write and perform their original songs?

A music program of the future would experiment with all these ideas, not just for the sake of novelty or to cater to the alternative crowd, but to include excellent music that supports the purpose and theme of the worship service.

The question of excellence must go beyond subjective matters of taste. Standards of musical excellence in worship may be difficult to define, but not impossible. In his book, *Beyond the Worship Wars*, seminary professor Thomas G. Long writes:

> ...the first mark of excellence in worship is a functional one. Good music is that which empowers the congregation and gives the congregation a means to express the thought and feelings of their worship. If a hymn or other musical piece is beyond a congregation's range or reach, then it cannot be called excellent, no matter how superb it may be on internal and technical grounds.

The key phrase here is "gives the congregation a means to express the thought and feelings of *their* [italics added] worship." The most important steps in developing a music program are to analyze the existing culture of a congregation, assess what style of music is not being offered, and then develop a plan for expanding the repertoire of musical possibilities.

Serving the theme and purpose of the worship service is easier to address. Because Unitarian Universalist worship services are not usually lectionary or Bible based, our worship leaders tend to look for music that will speak to the sermon or service theme or mood. The criteria to use when selecting such music includes tone, mood, style, and content. What tone does the music set? Is it written in a minor key—usually associated with the more thoughtful, internal, or disturbing emotions? Or is it in a major key— generally bright, energetic, and positive? Does the style fit with the overall theme and mood the leader is trying to create? For example, in a service commemorating the victims of the 2004 tsunami in Asia, what would be the impact if the music leader played Neil Young's "Like a Hurricane"? What if she played Handel's "Water Music"? A skillful and sensitive worship leader will consider the emotional weight of the style of music being considered for any given Sunday.

Finally, a worship leader or music director must consider the content of the music chosen. For example, a piece of high church liturgical music may be recognized as great but have a theology, such as sin or atonement, that is abhorrent to many UUs. Explaining its background to the congregation before it is performed may make it less theologically offensive. Often, when words to choral pieces are printed in the order of service, a context is also provided, placing this piece of music in a particular time and place. Most Unitarian Universalists seem to be open to all forms of classical music, as long as they are not expected to accept the theology presented.

When the subject of appropriate content to be played on Sunday morning came up in a worship class, Kathleen asked, "What kind of music should *not* be played in a Unitarian Universalist church?" People in the class struggled with the question, because it seemed to go against our democratic, free-speech principles. Kathleen pressed harder: "Should the 2006 Oscar-winning song, 'It's Hard Out Here for a Pimp?' be performed in a UU worship service? Is that inappropriate?"

The discussion turned to context, and the class agreed that almost any style or content of music could be played in a Unitarian Universalist church, but the congregation needed to know *why* a piece of music was selected and the purpose it was expected to serve.

The question facing Unitarian Universalists today should not be whether to include contemporary music, songs, and instruments, but how. Megachurches regularly create their own music for worship, and project the lyrics on a screen, thereby moving the musical focus up from the hymnal to looking together at the words. A few Unitarian Universalist churches are experimenting with their hymnody aids, using current technology such as a digital projector to project lyrics and artistic images. We like to imagine ourselves as part of the liturgical avant-garde, but the truth is that few Unitarian Universalists are on the cutting edge of creating musical offerings for worship in any genre. Even though many UUs are uncomfortable with Christian praise music, we must acknowledge the enormous power and appeal it has for the thousands of people who want music that is not foreign to their everyday lives.

This acknowledgment does not mean that we must abandon our classical music tradition to write the Unitarian Universalist equivalent of Christian praise music. Whether Unitarian Universalists prefer to sing William How's "For All the Saints," Carolyn McDade's "Spirit of Life," or Christine Tata's UU praise song "Holy Time," the purpose of congregational singing is for members to participate fully in the worship experience. The tunes may be familiar or new; they may be sung to the accompaniment of an organ, piano, or guitar. The ultimate goal is the same: the songs are meant to encourage robust congregational singing. This goal may be achieved by encouraging your congregation to sing without accompaniment, so they can truly hear each other's voices. It may mean investing in song leaders or cantors to help build a congregation's confidence in their singing, or holding hymn sings before the worship service or on the fifth Sunday of the month or as an adult class. Whatever the technique, our hope is that members will open their hymn books or read the words on a screen or sing a hymn from memory and realize that the act of singing provides both a comfort and a challenge to their ever-deepening involvement with the holy.

TIPS

- Have a conversation in your congregation about music in worship, and identify whether there are unacknowledged norms for music that the culture of the congregation enforces.

- Maintain standards of excellence in classical music, but consider exploring sacred themes from contemporary classical composers as well as older and more familiar ones.

- Encourage enthusiastic singing and leadership from the choir in all styles of music, seeing it as a gift to their fellow church members.

- Explore the values both musicians and members have around using recordings in worship. For smaller congregations without regular professional or volunteer musicians, recorded music may be mandatory, but for larger congregations practices vary. Recorded music, skillfully used in certain worship settings, expands the range of musical possibilities in worship.

• Find ways to expand the congregation's musical repertoire to include the best of world music, using *Singing the Living Tradition* and *Singing the Journey* as resources, but adding guest artists and recordings as opportunities arise.

• Identify contemporary musicians whose message is UU-friendly, and consider ways to integrate them into liturgy.

• Don't assume you must establish alternative music services; instead focus on integration of diverse music styles into Sunday mornings. Alternative worship services should reflect a different size of worship space and style of service, with musical genre as a component of the needs the service is designed to meet. Only the largest UU congregations have the ability to create a second or third worship service with a different music style as its primary distinguishing feature.

• If you are changing your musical baseline, whether in a new service or through conversion of an existing one, you will need to assemble a house band of professional and volunteer musicians to play regularly. Encourage them to write music for the church. If this is beyond your church's capacity, budget for guest musicians whose music speaks to Unitarian Universalists.

Prayers

When it comes to understanding the form and meaning of prayerful moments in Unitarian Universalist worship, the first practical question we encounter is our dilemma with the language of reverence.

One minister in a congregation we visited began her prayer, "Spirit of Life, Holy One, named and unnamed, mother and father of us all…" and the introduction continued for what seemed like a full minute. This style of opening prayer is not uncommon in Unitarian Universalist churches. Ministers are keenly aware that if they were simply to say "Dear God…" some members of their congregation would flinch in the moment or protest later. We strive to be as theologically inclusive as possible. We ask ourselves, what about the pagans in our midst? How do we include them in a spoken prayer? How about the atheists in our congregation, for whom the word *God* or the mention of a deity outside of human knowledge is meaningless? If we avoid the word *prayer* and the forms of prayer, and call that segment of the service "Meditation," we may recognize that the last thing the committed meditators in our pews do when they are meditating is listen to lengthy poetic exhortations. If these quiet and contemplative moments in our worship point toward a dependency on the mystery of life that is beyond our naming, how do the words and actions we choose to use help or hinder us in this task?

This is the unique dilemma of anyone who is supposed to lead the prayer time in a Unitarian Universalist congregation. In UU humor, the joke is that we pray "to whom it may concern," an approach generic enough to cover just about every theological persuasion. At the same time, the many poetic forms we use can create an invocation so bland or jumbled as to strip the prayer of any power or import. How can we pray with integrity, grace, power, and purpose, when we struggle with the question of to whom we are praying?

Many worship leaders who wish to address a reality larger than ourselves resolve the dilemma by using the most inclusive form they can. We noted earlier the popularity of "Spirit of Life" as a beginning for prayer because it represents a safe harbor for both theists and humanists.

Some of our churches use traditional prayer forms that have been part of their liturgies and congregational identities for generations. Inclusivity is a value for these congregations, but they will not compromise their liturgical identity and tradition to achieve it. Instead, they search for it outside the worship service. Most of our congregations give their ministers and worship leaders broad leeway in how they use and introduce prayers or meditations.

Our advice is to keep it simple. If you like to use diverse invocations, don't use them all in one prayer. Use ones that have both integrity in the context of your own theology and the potential to include the widest variety of people. As an alternative, begin with the same invocation every week, but let the congregation know what it means to you from your theological perspective and how you believe its consistent use adds to the worship life of the whole congregation.

The balance of words and silence is an important decision in whatever form of prayer or meditation you use. One of Kathleen's pet peeves occurs in both Unitarian Universalist churches and in other traditions. The minister says "Will you join me in a time of prayer or meditation?" and then launches into a long, wordy prayer that takes the listener to the other ends of the earth and heaven and back, ending with a prompt and efficient "Amen." Too often there is no time allowed for silence before or after the prayer. Prayer may be felt as just one more thing to be done before the sermon can begin.

The power of silence cannot be overestimated, and yet it is one of the aspects of liturgy most lacking in our worship. Perhaps this is because most of us are uncomfortable with silence. Our discomfort may come from our rebelling against having to be silent in church as children, or perhaps it is the awareness that when we enter silence together, we really aren't completely silent. The minister's stomach rumbles. A child cries in the back of the sanctuary. Someone coughs and another rustles through her purse to find a cough drop. It's difficult, if not impossible, to order complete silence on a Sunday morning in worship. We suspect that the more compelling reason that Unitarian Universalists tend to shun silence is that it invites us to enter deep waters of the spirit, and we do not know if we have the buoyancy to swim.

"Be still and know that I am God," the psalmist writes. And 1 Kings 19:12 says, "God was not in the fire, or in the earthquake, or in the wind, but in the still, small voice." To sit together in silence requires confronting the inner workings of our own minds. In silence, we see more clearly our thoughts and feelings, our hopes and losses. We can shut them out by compiling our to-do lists or fretting about the crying baby, but if we continue with the silence, we feel the tug of the spirit calling us to a larger life. For some, these feelings are strange and unsettling. There is nothing to do in that silence but "be." There are no landmarks, no roadmaps, no GPS systems to guide us, save for the rhythm of our own heartbeat and the rise and fall of our own breath.

A skillful prayer can provide a congregation with these landmarks and put a name to the feelings that well up in silence. It can guide beginning travelers through the emptiness of their own silence and help them to see the variety and beauty that exists there. Worship leaders whose prayers touch the congregation deeply and consistently are people whose prayers well up from their personal spiritual practice. The single most effective thing a person can do to create meaningful prayers is to have a rich private prayer life oneself. When a congregation enters a deeper silence together, the feeling in the room is palpable. The silence is rich and dense, as if all had just dived into a refreshingly clear lake on a hot summer day. It is here, in this space, that the knowing comes, that the insight is seen and the healing witnessed.

To make this possible, this silence can be neither too long nor too short. If it is too short, there is not enough time to delve deeply, but allows for skimming the surface. If it is too long, those meditating or praying may find their minds wandering far afield. The meditative stance should always be alert, awake, and receptive. The silence before, during, or after the prayer or spoken meditation is useful if it helps the individual move into the depths of their own being and then out again.

Prayer can cut through our intellectual barriers and touch our hearts, enabling us to feel truly held and embraced by community and by love. Led by a minister or worship leader who pulls a prewritten prayer from the hymnbook minutes before delivery, it can also leave us bored. At its best, prayer is a conversation between people and their minister, their community, the world, or their God.

The most meaningful prayers are not cleverly written but sincerely delivered. Cerebral prayers can leave us cold. The purpose of prayer is not to outline one's systematic theology; it is to put the mind and the heart together in a spirit of attentive, calm, and quiet awareness.

When a prayer does not contain a shred of the person who offers it, it is a hollow echoing of words, regardless of its poetry, craft, or style. The preacher or worship leader must know the congregation well enough to speak to their condition that day. "Canned" prayers seldom have the power of a prayer that has been born in the moment.

When prayers are poorly written or delivered in a preachy voice, it can distance us from the act of prayer. In theistic language, to pray is to make a humble presentation to God. It is an acknowledgment of our limitations, a statement of our hopes and longings, and a concession of our will. While there are no bad prayers, the poorly done prayer feels formulaic, ungraspable, and rushed.

The purpose of prayer in transformative worship is to allow enough silent time in the worship for transformation to occur. When we sit together in silence, when we lift up in prayer the gamut of human experience and emotion, we create a time to reflect on these things. When we are invited to a period of meditation and can focus on our breath or a word or an image, the action has the ability to distill our thoughts. When we can listen fully and reflectively to the "still small voice" within, we may be surprised and encouraged by what emerges.

TIPS

- Avoid overly intellectual prayers. Remember that prayer is not an opportunity to exercise your vocabulary. Prayer is conversation— know to whom or to what you are speaking.

- If you are asked to pray extemporaneously, or are struggling with how to write a prayer, there are four classic categories of prayer that can serve as a guide: adoration, confession, thanksgiving, and supplication. Keep them in mind by using the mnemonic device ACTS.

- The single most effective thing a person can do to create meaningful prayers is have a rich, private prayer life oneself. It is from this place of personal spiritual practice where deep prayer truly flows.

- If you are the person charged with the task of writing a prayer, allow time for silence both before and after the prayer. Listen deeply for the voice within and allow yourself to speak to that voice. Listen to preachers when they pray and analyze what it is about their tempo, pacing, articulation, and sense of authenticity that touches you. Then, try to incorporate those attributes into your own prayer.

- If incorporating formal meditation in the service in addition to your spoken meditation or prayer, announce the length of time you will be sitting and end the silent medition formally, with a bell sound or brief closing words.

Meditations

Many UU churches include meditation as part of the service or in place of prayer. Meditation can take at least two forms; it can be the practice of sitting silently and either counting one's breath or allowing thoughts to rise and fall away, or it can refer to a guided meditation that is led by the worship leader. Both forms can be effective in stilling the mind and calming our restless spirits, but there are important caveats to consider.

To engage in meditation together, people are likely to need some instruction. Most will have some intellectual knowledge of meditation, but little actual practice. Suggestions may include an invitation to get comfortable, followed by counting one's breaths in and out up to ten, and beginning again with one. Remind people that thoughts will arise, some trivial and others troubling, but the point is to notice those thoughts, release them, and return to focusing on one's breath. Also tell people that you will frame the meditation time with a bell sound, or some other signal. Follow the meditation time with something soothing, such as soft music or a poem, to gently welcome people back into the present.

In guided meditation, the leader takes the congregation on a journey. The journey may be through one's own body, or exploring the past, or connecting to the vastness of the universe. It can work very well if given enough time, but too often leaders hurry through the meditation, leaving the people in the pews feeling rushed and frustrated. Guided meditations can be powerfully evocative and may inadvertently bring about an emotional reaction. For example, on a Sunday when youth was the focus of the service, the worship leader decided to lead the congregation on a trip from their childhood to adolescence. At least two people later reported to the minister that they had been sexually or emotionally abused in the past and that the meditation, while meant to be a joyful journey through childhood, was an excruciating exercise.

Guided meditations should not be used too often, but reserved for times when they would have a positive and deepening effect on the congregation. For example, in services that have themes related to "imagination," or "creativity," or "journey," we could imagine effectively using a guided meditation that engaged people with imagery or with their memories as a means to enhance the experience of the theme. The meditations should be carefully written, reviewed by another worship leader or minister, and given enough time to be meaningful. Finally, the leader might want to have resources available for those who took seriously the challenge to go deeper into the meditation and now need to find a way to cope with what emerged.

Regardless of what one's particular congregation calls this time, there should be, at a given point in the service, some time to simply be together in silence. Silence nourishes and sustains us. It creates surprising bonds of trust. It gives voice to our deepest longings, our inchoate fears, our great joys. The regular, weekly practice of meditation, reflection, or prayer is worth every word not spoken.

TIPS

- Provide intervals of silence when speaking the words you use to introduce or weave through the meditation.

- Include several stages of instruction in a guided meditation. Small steps will allow people to better experience the journey.

- Don't make assumptions about people's past or current experiences in guided meditation.

- Consider the possibility of occasional Buddhist meditation in your worship: three to ten minutes of silent sitting with brief instruction on focusing on the breath.

Joys and Concerns

Open-ended invitations to express joys and concerns during the service are a cherished part of the liturgy in many UU congregations. Whatever the criticisms or abuses that arise from time to time, the power of this ritual of personal sharing embodies what many UUs hold up as one of our most important principles and hallmarks of our approach to church: the use of the democratic process within our congregations. Some ministers or lay worship leaders who have suggested abandoning the ritual came away feeling like they touched a third rail in the life of the congregation.

Many congregations have sought a creative compromise between an open-ended invitation and elimination of the ritual altogether. In discussing alternative approaches, it is important to point the conversation away from being about democracy and authority, and toward being about how the pastoral ministry of the congregation can be acknowledged in worship. Even in small congregations there is no way that all the pastoral issues and personal feelings of those present will be expressed through a Joys and Concerns ritual. It will always be a sampling from people who are the most motivated and expressive. The idea that it is a sampling makes it easier to understand the ritual as having a symbolic role in the liturgy, rather than a functional one. There are better ways for the congregation's pastoral ministry leaders to hear about something going on in a member's life than a public announcement in worship.

Some of the following innovations in Joys and Concerns rituals are intended to address particular problems, while others seek to replace the spoken ritual with liturgical or prayerful responses from the worship leaders.

Setting Time Limits: The invitation to come forward includes a reminder that the time for this element of the service is limited to, for example, five minutes. People are asked to line up and if time runs out, those still in line will not be able to speak.

Locating Joys and Concerns After the Sermon: To avoid having an especially lengthy or intense session detract from the sermon, the ritual is located after the sermon. This has both the advantage and disadvantage of encouraging joys or concerns that are sermon-responsive, as well as those that arise from the lives of congregation members. The advantage of this approach is that if the service has run long, or there are many people wishing to speak, the congregation as a whole is given responsibility for how long the service will continue, rather than the worship leader. People who have reached the limits of their available time can choose to leave during the ritual, knowing it's near the end of the service.

Having a Silent Candle Lighting: The lighting may be accompanied by music, by the chalice lighting, or by a pulpit prayer or meditation that speaks generally to the pastoral needs of the people. The physical act of coming forward to light a candle in front of the congregation invites other members to ask the reason for the candle, if it is not well known.

Acknowledging Milestones: The title of this form of Joys and Concerns suggests to the congregation that this time is more for major life events than broad social concerns or expressions of gratitude.

Offering a Book of Life: A sizeable blank Book of Life is stationed at the entrance to the worship space, possibly accompanied by an array of candles. The joys and concerns are written there, and a candle is lit, without the expectation that the written text will be spoken out loud in the service. The book is then available to encourage follow-up by the pastoral ministry team.

Embracing Meditation: Before or during the service, candles may be lit, with an invitation to write one's joy or concern on a piece of paper. A worship associate or the worship leader then puts these notes in an order that allows them to be mentioned in an embracing meditation or prayer. Some worship leaders mention people by name, while others combine the notes in more general petitions without mentioning names.

Inviting Prayers of the People: During the major prayer, the worship leader invites the congregation to vocalize their own prayers. A suggested form for beginning or ending these prayers can be provided in the order of service. It might include a congregational unison response to each prayer. Having someone model the length and form of the prayer by speaking first gives people an immediate example of what is expected. For example, the minister invites the prayers of the people with the words: "Let us now speak the prayers that are in our hearts." People respond in the following format: "For the continued recovery of my mother-in-law Connie as she comes back from the stroke she suffered last month." The congregation then answers in unison: "We hold Connie in our hearts," or "Let this be our prayer," or something similar. When no one else wishes to initiate a prayer, the worship leader concludes with: "For all those prayers that are too great or too small to have found voice today, we hold them in our hearts."

Including pastoral concerns in the order of service: Some congregations that don't use a Joys and Concerns ritual are careful to include news and updates on pastoral concerns within the congregation in the order of service. Some congregations also use the chalice lighting as an occasion in the service for announcements of deaths, awards, or other milestones.

TIPS

- Educate the congregation about the purpose of Joys and Concerns, making clear that it is not a time for announcements, political statements, or recruitment of people for committees or coffee hour.

- Experiment with a variety of styles until you find the one that will work well over time.

- Find ways for your congregation to connect other than through Joys and Concerns—for example, through small group ministry, a Joys and Concerns column in the newsletter, or pastoral visitors.

Readings

In our preaching careers, we have had at least three different approaches to choosing the readings: They are selected as adornments, companions, or spiritual guides.

Adornment readings can be scriptures, poetry, or prose. Used to introduce or foreshadow the sermon's main message, they may or may not be referred to in the sermon. They are often included to fill a slot in the order of service, but if they were eliminated, the sermon would not suffer in clarity or strength. Adornment readings can be chosen after a sermon has been fully conceived or even written. Rerun sermons that are being offered by guest ministers can be accompanied by adornment readings that are required by the occasion and by the location for the second preaching of the sermon being different from the first.

Readings that are companions are an integral part of the sermon, cited because they make a point that the preacher wants to hold up strongly but not claim as an original idea. These selections, particularly scriptural readings, may contain a story that the sermon will reference or elucidate. Presumably each could stand alone. A sermon could make reference to a companion reading or even quote some of it, without the reading occupying its own line in the order of service. A companion reading could convey important meanings in a worship service that had no sermon or homily. Hand in hand in one service, however, the reading and sermon are each made stronger.

These first two approaches to choosing readings stand in contrast to treating the reading as a spiritual guide. This practice is akin to lectionary preaching and has been used and advocated by some of our leading preachers. (See "The Sermon" on choosing readings as spiritual guides.)

TIPS

- Know how your readings will serve the service—whether as adornments, companions, or spiritual guides.

- Don't choose readings that are too long or intellectually dense. The meaning of the readings should be easily grasped by the majority of the congregation.

- Be careful not to overuse a particular author or poet (e.g., Robert Fulghum or Mary Oliver).

- Make regular reading part of your spiritual practice to build up your own library of good material for readings.

- Practice your readings out loud. Read for weight, meaning, musical intonation, and poetry. If possible, read to another person and ask for feedback about clarity of meaning and vocal tone.

- Remember that the reading in Unitarian Universalist churches often takes the place of Biblical scripture. Make sure your reading is worthy of such an esteemed place in the liturgy.

Sermons

"I love to tell the story" begins a favorite gospel hymn, and the sermon in transformational worship does tell a story. The sermons we each submitted that both won Borden Sermon Prizes in 2003 were very different, but both were completely built around vivid stories and images. One began with a dramatic confrontation in an airline counter ticket line, and an internal struggle about whether to get involved. The other interwove the experience of witnessing an autopsy, reflecting on body, soul, and the experience of God. Sermons that tell a story are by no means light on intellectual argument.

Most preachers will tell you that parishioners who comment specifically on a certain part of a sermon will usually share their response to a story or image it included. Their reasons for doing so are not always the same. Sometimes the story reminds them of a time in their own lives when something similar happened to them. Sometimes it touches deeply held values and the emotions associated with them, even when it does not describe an experience that has any parallel in their own lives. Sometimes the story is just captivating, because it is vividly told, or has a twist or a moral that grabs their attention. People will often ask us for a copy of the text of our sermon when they want to review how it was structured as an argument, but that is usually because a story helped the message get through to them.

Many churches have initiated a worship associates program for training the laity in the liturgical arts. The piece of their training that many worship associates have the most angst about is writing a sermon. They exclaim, "I can fill five minutes of time—but twenty! What do I say?" Or they confidently stride into our office with a fifteen-page, single-spaced manuscript on a topic appropriate to a university lectern rather than the free pulpit.

Much has already been written in our own denomination about what makes for excellence in preaching, and there are some definite hallmarks of a good sermon. It is in large part more art than craft. In that respect, no book can teach you to be an excellent preacher. There are some qualities necessary for excellent preaching that cannot be taught, such as an ear for language, a sense of musicality and timing, and the ability to take listeners on a twenty-minute journey that leaves them in a better place than when they arrived.

REVERSE TIPS

For many years, the Revs. Jane Rzepka and Ken Sawyer led a popular preaching seminar for UU ministers. Among the resources they gave their students was a list of reverse tips for giving a truly terrible sermon, an exhaustive collection of the worst preaching practices found in Unitarian Universalism today:

• Make it longer than they expect. Long before the end say, "In con-clusion...."

• Preach mostly about yourself.

• Mumble.

• Assume that you are more spiritually evolved than they are. Try to bring them along.

• Ignore the service around the sermon.

- Choose a topic that only you care about.

- Use crude language.

- Exclude some parishioners with your theology.

- Have no religious point.

- Tell a personal story about someone without his or her permission.

- Count on inspiration to show up when you want it to.

- Don't acknowledge Unitarian Universalism.

- Preach without including any actual ideas.

- Toss in lots and lots of images, stories, and quotes, as many as you can.

- Assume that good grammar is for the faint of heart.

- Apologize.

- Give a book report.

- Assume that the sermon will carry itself without need of stories or humor.

- Be sure to show off your impressive vocabulary.

- Preach generic sermons, ignoring local context and world events.

- Presume that everyone there shares the same assumptions, experience, background, politics, and level of privilege.

- Brag. Make the star of the crucial story, you.

- No one cares if you can't really sing; break into song in the midst of your sermon.

- Use a string of clichés.

- Don't look at anyone, or stare at only a person or two.

- Gratuitous manipulation of people's feelings is always appreciated.

- Whine.

- Keep them abreast of your children and pets with amusing tales.

- Wait until the last minute to print your sermon.

- If your point is weak, pound the pulpit.

- Play with the change in your pockets.

- Use huge amounts of time to tell how brief you'll be.

- Dress seductively.

- Use very long quotes and be unclear about when they begin and end.

- Focus on delivering a great sermon rather than speaking to the hearts and minds of your parishioners.

Intergenerational Worship

Making the shift to a different frequency and style of intergenerational worship at West Shore Church has required a lot of our worship leaders and congregation. We went from the story-for-all-ages format to monthly full intergenerational services. Lifespan Faith Development Director Kathy Strawser and Sabbatical Minister Tamara Lebak used the church's media to prepare the way, engaging the congregation about their own discomforts, fears, and preferences through articles in our monthly newsletter and also the family newsletter for those enrolled in religious education classes.

Articles alone would not have been enough to create the kind of engagement necessary. Kathy also prepared two skits that were offered in the worship services on the Sundays leading up to the first full intergenerational services. The first brought out the concerns of a young parent about what it would mean to attend church services with children in tow. The second depicted the concerns of an older church member who had never had children, as she imagined what it would be like to experience the entire service with children present.

The skits were scripted in a conversational format, with good humor and insightful advice about how to deal with the discomforts that might be involved. Both characters were given speeches where they reflected on some of the positive possibilities and advantages of coming to church all together. Because the skits portrayed both the concerns and the possibilities that existed across the age spectrum, the congregation saw that these services were being planned with everyone in mind.

Recognizing that there would be people who came to services without realizing that the entire hour would be intergenerational, Kathy created a pamphlet called "Worshiping Together," which shared some of the philosophy of intergenerational worship at our church and gave advice for how to make the worship experience work for all ages.

When our initial experiment with routine intergenerational worship in our social hall was over we prepared the way for moving the intergenerational format into our 350-seat sanctuary. The larger space and the fixed pews meant everyone was more spread out than they had been in the social hall. The pamphlet was rewritten to reflect the new realities of the sanctuary worship. Services were announced well in advance through the monthly newsletter so that everyone who paid attention to the church media knew what to expect.

Planning and leading an hour-long intergenerational worship service begins with the recognition that it is not going to be children's worship. To be truly intergenerational, the service must speak to people of different ages through different layers of meaning contained within the same element of worship. This had always been our best hope for the story for all ages: that it would be a story with a message not only for children but adults as well. However, looking at all the elements of the service with this same lens, seeing how they can connect with people of different ages, makes new demands on worship planners.

Begin with the theme of the service. Thematic worship series have become common in many Protestant worship traditions. These themes may connect with the flow of the liturgical year but they can also be inspired by events in the life of the church or the larger world. The All Souls Unitarian Church in Tulsa, Oklahoma, has developed a model of theme-based intergenerational church life, in which a rotation of monthly themes about the great questions and issues of religious life engages everyone. Worship services, religious education classes for all ages, and small-group ministries take up the month's theme in different ways. Even without such a comprehensive approach, we can consider themes that will be a bridge between children's worship and the adult service, or that will provide a platform for a fully intergenerational Sunday morning service.

Keeping the theme visible and connected throughout all the sections of the service can help layer the meanings in your service. The different elements of worship speak to us all through different modes of learning, different senses, different sides of our brains. The service themes need to be explored in all the modes and opportunities a worship service offers if it is to speak to all the ages that are present. Children especially are sensitive to differences between what is said and what is done. If the actions they see as part of the service do not match the words, there is a layer of meaning and learning conveyed that may not be what was intended, but is nonetheless true. So for example, if children see the offering plate being passed, but also see their parents or other people letting it go by without putting something in it, they are likely to wonder how this matches up with what they are being taught about generosity and service.

The separate elements of worship have the potential to speak to us all through different modes of learning. Unitarian Universalist worship over the past fifty years has strongly emphasized the auditory and intellectual modes. Other senses are not absent, but are much less engaged. Younger people learn at school using more visual and tactile modalities than we are accustomed to including in our worship, and energetic young bodies get restless sitting still for an hour. Finding ways to engage as many of the senses as possible when leading intergenerational worship will be a delight for all ages.

We advocated strongly for a digital projector to enhance our services, especially the intergenerational ones. Generous gifts through a special appeal made it possible to install a projector and be able to use PowerPoint or DVD images in worship whenever we want. It seemed obvious that using visual images to illustrate stories in intergenerational services would be a good idea, and they were well received. The days of holding up a book with pictures that even the children sitting nearby can barely see are gone.

However, it was intriguing to see the adult response when we tried using more extensive PowerPoint presentations to complement a sermon outside of intergenerational worship. Many people felt we had gone overboard on the visual component. Consistent imagery behind the sermon was experienced as distracting, especially by those who identified as auditory learners. In response, we've struck a balance by finding the places in any service where a visual component will bring some unique added value.

In our fixed-pew sanctuary, we've also looked for new ways to create routine movement in the service. Standing for hymns and songs was our most typical movement. Now, most weeks, we invite people to find someone they don't know in the sanctuary and greet that person. We also try to have segments of the congregation, especially the children during intergenerational services, engage in a ritual activity that involves the need to get up and move. Candle-lighting rituals, creating chalices on felt boards, and the Japanese practice of tying a prayer note to a string have all been service elements for us. We also use gestures to accompany some of our covenants and chalice lightings.

Vicarious movement is helpful when there are periods of time in the service that require the congregation to remain seated. The way the minister or speaker uses movement during the sermon or the inclusion of artists, such as dancers, can be important vehicles for keeping all ages engaged.

Your creativity can be the only limitation on the possibilities for a broader engagement of as many senses as possible during a time of intergenerational worship. At the Cedar Ridge Community Church in Spencerville, Maryland, we encountered a new way to think about communion time that offers possibilities for UU intergenerational worship. This congregation had a number of stations and suggestions for how people engage with the communion time. They could take communion in the traditional way, by themselves, with the minister, or with their family or friends around a table. They could also use the communion time for a devotional practice such a candle or incense lighting or prayer writing, both practice modes that are easy for children to engage. Handling meditative objects, walking prayer, or meditation were possibilities as well.

During our experiment with a full schedule of intergenerational worship, our choir was asked to participate in the service in a different way. Our choir has a featured anthem in most services, and offers introits, prayer responses, and choral benedictions less frequently. Tamara and Kathy felt that the choral music would be more accessible to all ages if the choir focused on the shorter pieces that brought a thread of continuity and thematic emphasis to the liturgy at strategic points. Where longer anthems were used, it was because they illuminated the overall service theme. Choir members were regularly asked to be song leaders, which was easier to do in the social hall because they were not sitting in the choir loft. The debut of the 2005 hymnal supplement gave us many new rounds, chants, and praise songs to try out, and many of these were very appropriate for the intergenerational format. We learned a lot during that time that has been incorporated into the monthly intergenerational services that occur in our larger sanctuary.

Two words come to mind when considering how to use both musical and homiletic elements to create transformative intergenerational worship: *short* and *dense*. *Short* refers to songs whose words and length allow all ages to easily enter and stick with the experience of singing or listening. The pacing of intergenerational worship is important. Keeping all the elements moving along, with fewer verses and briefer readings, can make a big difference. Plain language—simple but not necessarily simplistic—can convey multilayered depth. Simple rhythms build participation and enjoyment. Our hymnbooks and those of other traditions have some rich musical resources for shorter hymns, rounds, and chants from many of the world's religious traditions. Avoid the four-verse nineteenth-century hymns with complex images and words. Consider instead using verses from popular music that are familiar to most people. Don't be afraid to include time for learning new songs before a service begins and to repeat songs that all ages are beginning to learn by heart.

Density refers to the quality of multiple meaning. A round like "Gathered Here in the Mystery of the Hour" is not hard to sing, has words most children can understand, engages everyone in a compelling rhythm, and has a density that can touch the heart differently from person to person and week to week. Images in both songs and sermons can have both literal and figurative meanings that have value for different kinds of parishioners.

When we began to prepare sermons for these intergenerational services, we decided to break them into two or three parts to accomodate younger attention spans. We quickly got feedback from our members that older attention spans found these sermons more accessible as well. Unitarian Universalists resist the fill-in-the-blank sermon guides often included in the bulletins that evangelical congregations distribute on Sundays. To most of our members, it feels insulting to be asked to come up with the key word in a sentence that is one of the central points of the sermon, and then write that word in a blank space on an insert. However, for intergenerational Sundays, this kind of insert would be accepted and understood by most congregations as a great device for keeping children focused, and many adults would also use it. A sermon broken into sections, with separate titles listed in the order of service to convey the main point for each, can also help people of all ages engage with and retain the sermon more completely.

Symbolic props can be another helpful device. Shorter sermon segments associated with a prop can include and hold some density for adults, while offering a hook that children can hang on to, helping them take home a learning or a moral lesson associated with that symbol. A good story can serve this purpose, providing the hook for everyone—children will retain the sermon's meaning and adults will add to the story some of the density that invites further conversation or contemplation.

Try to make the songs and homiletic elements connect themati-
cally, so the main points of the service are repeated and reaffirmed
in these different learning modes. A message that is sung can stick in
the mind of a child or an adult in ways that the same message heard
through a sermon will not.

Despite all these efforts to include people of all ages in the worship
experience, we also make available activity boxes for younger children
in the services. Having crayons and images to color or puzzles to
work on can fill the time when a child isn't able to stay engaged. These
activity boxes in themselves can be an opportunity for reinforcing
the theme of the service; it's not to hard to find images to color that
can provide one more connection to the message you are trying to
convey.

TIPS

- Prepare the congregation for intergenerational worship with advance announcements about whether children will attend the full
  service, or only a part of it.

- Have clear expectations, guidelines, and support for families with
  restless children.

- Have an accessible theme that is connected to all parts of the
  service.

- Express the theme of the service through the use of as many senses
  as possible.

- Use movement, ritual, props, and/or audiovisuals in the service.

- Consider shorter hymn choices with easily pronounced words and
  simple rhythms.

- Find ways to convey meanings on many levels that work for diverse
  ages. Don't expect that the service has to be geared to a second-
  grade level, but think about how younger children will be able to
  engage.

- Have activity boxes available in the pews or seats for children who have trouble staying engaged.

Honoring and Respecting Our World's Cultures

Unitarian Universalist worship is enriched and enlivened by the use of ritual, readings, sermon resources, and music from around the world. Worship leaders who use such elements intentionally and thoughtfully, rather than randomly and casually, are not just modeling transformative worship; they are also embodying anti-racist, anti-oppressive understandings in this important public context for multicultural education and celebration.

Over the last decade, Unitarian Universalist educators have shown us how to ask the right questions as we seek to honor and experience diverse traditions in our worship services in a respectful and non-oppressive manner.

At the 2001 General Assembly in Cleveland, Jacqui James presented a list of questions that should come up in our soul searching about cultural borrowing. Her work formed a basis for many other articles and reflections that followed. We find seven of her questions, paraphrased here, particularly relevant for planning worship with multicultural content:

- How much do I know about this particular tradition? How do I respect it and not misrepresent it?

- What do I know of the history and experience of the people from whom I am borrowing?

- Does this borrowing distort, water down, or misinterpret the tradition?

- Am I changing the meaning?

- Am I overgeneralizing this culture? (Remind yourself that any culture can be quite diverse.)

- What is the motivation for this borrowing? What is being sought and why?

- How do the "owners" of the tradition feel about pieces of the tradition being borrowed?

Exhaustive answers to all these questions is not the point. The point is to be aware of the broader implications of the choices you make in putting a worship service together. If your honest answers to some of these questions above lean towards "I don't know" or "No," you have work to do before you can appropriately include the element in question in your worship.

In 2003, a UUA Cultural (Mis)Appropriations Ad Hoc Committee led by Director of Lifespan Faith Development Judith Frediani published another extensive and well-organized list of questions to help Unitarian Universalists determine when and how cultural borrowing is appropriate or possible. We recommend it to you and list it in the "Resources" section.

The Internet has made it easier to learn about the cultural context and meanings of a ritual or piece of music than ever before. But nothing can substitute for direct engagement with people who are part of or who have lived in the culture that you would like to engage or from which you want to borrow. This isn't always possible, although we live in a country that is more multicultural than ever before. The white suburban enclaves in which so many UU churches are located are increasingly our society's ghettoes of mono-culturalism. So it may take stepping outside familiar contacts and comfort zones to truly understand the context for the element you wish to use.

Unitarian Universalists have available to us a feast of sources of information for multicultural worship. As we consider who we are as Unitarian Universalists, and what Unitarian Universalist worship can include, it is important to remember that "we" are more diverse than we might think if we only look at the visible dominant cultures in our congregations. We are not just guests at this table. It is our table to claim and our feast to enjoy, but we must honor what we find laid before us with respect and appreciation.

The Liberal Religious Educators Association offers the following advice to presenters of worship services or conference programs:

TIPS

- Develop your program, workshop, or worship, not in isolation but in consultation with persons, communities, or religious groups whose culture is referenced in your presentation.

- Be mindful of the possible negative impact of cultural appropriation (enacting rituals or using stories, songs, objects, or symbols that are sacred to a particular culture). When in doubt, consult with a representative of that group about using such materials. Be particularly cautious when representatives of a community advise against using their traditions or materials.

- When you plan to share wisdom or information from a culture other than your own, credit your sources and place your story/activity in context, explaining why and how you have chosen to use the material.

- Include contemporary readings that represent cultures featured in your program, not limiting yourself to "long ago" materials. Use of only "long ago" materials and prayers can perpetuate the myth that certain cultures are from the past rather than the present.

CONCLUSION

We started our cross-country road trip with the hope of finding worship that works, worship that transforms the lives of worshipers. We thought that we could experience and name the transformative moments of successful worship. Was it the moment in a Roman Catholic service when the bread and wine become the body of Christ? Was it the euphoric high one gets when worshipping in a Pentecostal congregation that sways with a contemporary music, singing chant-like praise songs? Was it the chance to move one's body around a circular worship space in a chancel dance? Was it the powerfully preached sermon that engages mind, heart, and spirit?

We discovered that it can be any and all of these things—and none of them. We learned that transformation can and does happen in every worship experience, but it is both keenly subjective and overtly objective. There are some qualities and practices that help make transformative worship possible, and there are also some aspects that are unexplained, and ultimately unexplainable. Over the course of our sabbatical, and indeed throughout our lives as worship leaders and attendees, we have encountered moments when the practice of worship intersected with the experience of grace. Exploring that intersection can help us to understand transformative worship.

Spiritual practice outside of traditional church life has become more popular in the United States. Thousands flock to yoga studios, meditation groups, and contemplative prayer classes. People are awakening to the fact that some kind of spiritual practice—a regular activity dedicated to connecting them to the transcendent dimension of life, however they name that dimension—is an important discipline. For unchurched spiritually minded people, going to church has the chance to become their weekly form of spiritual practice, although they may not think of it that way at first. If such people are coming to worship hoping to connect more deeply with themselves, with others, and with the holy, our liturgical leaders are the people who prepare a room for them.

To experience transformative worship the first thing one has to do is show up, but it takes awhile to settle into the experience of worship. First-, second-, and third-time visitors are still tourists, just as we were when we traveled from place to place seeking transformative worship. We quickly realized that although we had often been touched and moved by the experience of worship in UU congregations, we were less likely to have that experience as observers at other traditions' church services. We took notes and analyzed our experiences instead of fully surrendering ourselves to the worship experience.

Although many of the evangelical and megachurch services have been explicitly designed for the Sunday morning seeker, these services often feel like a performance for the benefit of the first-time visitor. As we traveled, we remembered that there is no substitute for worshipping with others in a covenanted community—knowing that the depth, beauty, and meaning of rituals are created by and for a worshipping community that assembles each week.

Keeping in mind the centrality of a covenanted community, we nevertheless believe that there are practices of worship leadership and participation that help us find the graceful moments of transformation and make them more possible for everyone who attends. We recognize that such practices are the worship equivalent of practicing scales on a piano. They must be mastered to achieve excellence, but they do not guarantee a transformative experience for everyone.

During the period of our sabbatical research, a group of UU leaders in the Mid-South District began the "Excellence in Worship" project. They sent out a survey to UU ministers who had a reputation for excellence in worship, asking, among other questions: What makes worship excellent? How did you learn to lead excellent worship? What are the best and worst practices among us?

Based on the raw data in the survey findings, which were compiled by Starr King Seminarian Sally Hamlin, and our own experiences as worship attendees, leaders, and teachers, there are four components of excellent transformational worship that we would raise up for consideration: the story of the gathered community is always told; the leader and congregation are willing to risk encountering the sacred; the integrity, coherence, and the wholeness of the service embodies these possibilities in personal and communal life; and careful planning opens a door for grace. Let's look at each of these components:

The story of the gathered community is always told. In the survey report, our colleague Alice Blair Wesley writes: "A key element of a corporate identity is a sacred story linking past, present and future, a story of the group's 'whence and whither.' A worshipping community knows from whence we have come, what we have brought with us, from the past and that we yet treasure, what new things are asked of us now ... and therefore, where we are headed." Christian worship is a weekly reenactment of one of the world's greatest stories. Unitarian Universalist worship combines both our Protestant heritage and the stories from world religions to create a religious story that is uniquely our own. Furthermore, the history of our forebears, the Unitarians and the Universalists, is part of the story of the gathered community, which bears retelling time and time again. We do this in worship to remind ourselves of the firm roots of liberal religion upon which we stand. We hear the story of our gathered community each week to give us both roots and wings: to ground us in the past through ritual, storytelling, and song, and to free our spirits to prosper in the present and future.

The leader and congregation are willing to risk encountering the sacred. We suspect that at the heart of the worship experience is fear. Although this may sound decidedly not a UU idea, it's not an inappropriate response to the holy. When we find ourselves in the presence of the holy, it can be both awe-inspiring and terrifying. It is a landscape in which we do not dwell daily, and our initial response to that which is foreign to us is fear. At the same time, to encounter the sacred breaks up the hard clots of our ego, our resistance to grace, and moves us into a deeper and wider stream of life. When we encounter the sacred, we feel ourselves moving more freely, less encumbered by our own small selves. A well-planned, thoughtful, and artistically created liturgy can create the space where the self meets the sacred. However, the likelihood of that encounter is greatly reduced if both worship leader and congregation are unwilling to risk it.

Perhaps the foremost kind of risk is for the worship leaders to reach deeply and introspectively into their own souls to find the intersection of the ordinary and the sacred. The quality of their own inner lives has a direct impact on how willing leaders are to encounter the sacred in worship. Leaders must know that they can fall into the hands of the living God, and survive the encounter. They must know that they can face the darkest hours of the human spirit without collapsing into it. That confidence is born from daily spiritual practice and engagement with the holy through study, reflection, prayer, and other practices.

Assuming that leaders are prepared to take risks in worship, how does one prepare the congregation for that encounter, one that cannot be created on demand or on schedule? For a congregation to step onto holy ground, church attendees must feel safe. *Safe* is a word that is broadly used these days; in this context it means that the congregation trusts both the liturgy and the worship leaders. To create that trust, worship planners must carefully think through the emotional flow of the service. They might ask: Is the service planned to accommodate silence and introspection as well as participation and praise? How are transitions between sections of the liturgy handled? Are the participants asked to shift abruptly from their emotional selves to their intellectual selves to their social-justice selves? Is there time to "feel" in the service and if there is, is it handled with care? Is there anything emotionally manipulative in the service? These are all extremely subtle aspects of the liturgy, but when they are handled badly or not at all, they create a sense of inner dissonance that contributes to the feeling of not being safe in worship.

Creating a place to encounter the holy during worship also requires the worship leader to invite risk-taking from the congregation, acknowledging that people are touched in different ways. Some may respond to a Gregorian chant in a resonant sanctuary; others may find their hearts pounding to the rhythm of African drums. Some may find coming forward to light candles of joy or concern feels like an enormous risk, while others may find saying a prayer out loud as a group is both a challenge and a comfort. Excellence in worship is created by balancing the elements of risk and spontaneity with careful planning and predictability. A liturgy that is both comfortable because it is familiar and risky because it is new provides the best opportunity for transformative worship.

The service embodies the possibilities for integrity, coherence, and wholeness in personal and communal life. UU congregations, no matter how well-established they are in their worship practices and traditions, will always have an uphill battle overcoming congregational perceptions that the service is somehow about performance, affirming the institutional church, or entertainment. There will always be visitors and occasional attendees in every service. There will be people who came primarily to be with their friends and look to the time before and after worship as their real church time.

At every service, however, there are people who count on the worship experience to be their central spiritual practice each week. They come looking for encouragement in their own struggles to live lives that are rooted in their deepest values. They come seeking courage to do hard things, and not just for reassurance that they are OK the way they are (as important as that message is to convey at times). They come to understand their place in the larger story, traditions, and possibilities of the liberal religious life and community.

The burden for meeting those needs falls not just on the preacher or the sermon, but also on the integrity, coherence, and wholeness of the entire worship service. We believe that each Sunday our worship services should present a multidimensional picture of what it means to practice the liberal religious way of life. That picture is not a snapshot, however. A snapshot picture is more like the sermon title or theme posted on the sign outside the church. The experience of the worship service is more like a hologram than a snapshot of a liberal religious life. A hologram is most simply defined as a three-dimensional photograph. Many people have seen them in theme park attractions. Laser light shone through any small piece of a holographic image will reveal the whole image. Unlike the pieces of a snapshot, each piece of a hologram contains the whole, reminding us that each small piece of worship can contain and speak to all the longings that brought people to church that day. Perhaps you have attended a service that missed the mark for you on that particular day, except for the prayer, the music, and one of the readings. The exceptions in this case point to the rule. Any one segment of the service can invoke or embody the liberal religious life. Every piece of the worship service is important, and individual pieces become even more important and powerful if thought and planning is given to how they relate to the rest of the service.

This kind of careful planning and creativity makes a transformative worship experience possible for some people attending services on any given Sunday. Over time, however, the quality of worship life that is created with this kind of care is transformative for the entire congregation. It will result in a congregation whose members retain their diverse theologies but are more comfortable and literate in the languages of spiritual experience and commitment. It will result in a congregation where people still have differing relationships of spiritual practice, but are more broadly accepting and understanding of spiritual practice as a dimension of religious living. It will result in a congregation where political opinions and commitments differ, but whose prophetic witness is understood to be grounded in a person's whole life and how it is lived with integrity and purpose.

Careful planning opens a door for grace. Louis Pasteur said, "Chance favors the prepared mind." Likewise, grace, or the transformative moment in worship, when one's heart is strangely warmed to a new reality, is more likely to happen when worship leaders have carefully planned the liturgy. In all the churches where we experienced a moment of transformation, we did so because of the beauty, exactness, and intentionality of the liturgy and worship ritual. At St. Peter's Church in Cleveland, we were moved in body and spirit as we sat, sang, stood, walked to the communion table and baptismal font, were blessed by incense, and listened to ancient words read anew. At All Souls Church, Unitarian, in Washington, D.C., we were completely absorbed in the beauty and artistic perfection of the music, the visual art, and liturgical dance, as well as excellent preaching and high-church ritual. At the Vineyard Community Church outside of Cincinnati, we were touched by the video testimonials given by those who were going to be baptized that day. At the 11:11 service at First United Methodist Church in Fort Worth, Texas, we were deeply moved to hear a favorite Grateful Dead song, "Ripple," become a liturgical response that the congregation knew by heart. Behind the transformative moments we experienced there were hours of careful planning and preparation. In all these experiences, what made the difference were both a well-prepared and flawlessly enacted ritual and the sense that the ritual was organic to the ethos of the congregation. In essence, the combination of both excellence in preparing for worship and authenticity of practice made the experience special to even the casual, first-time visitor.

In his book, *The Varieties of Religious Experience*, William James writes,

> Were one asked to characterize the life of religion in the broadest and most general terms possible, one might say that it consists of the belief that there is an unseen order, and that our supreme good lies in harmoniously adjusting ourselves thereto....

What really happens in the worship experience? Regardless of one's theological orientation—humanist, theist, Buddhist, pagan—there is often an unspoken encounter with an unseen order. For the theist, that order is the reality of God. For the Buddhist, it is an awareness of no separation between self and everything else. For the humanist, it may be acknowledging our individual roles in the larger body of humanity. For the pagan, it is the spiritual reality within the natural world. Wherever one places one's faith, the deepest experience that happens in worship is often unseen. A worship leader can follow the prescribed steps in preparing for worship, and the result can still be uninspiring. The candles can be lit, the incense smoldering, the words written down carefully, the scripture thoughtfully exegeted—and there can still be no transformative moment in the service.

James has a partial explanation for the transformative worship moment: "Such objects may be present to our senses, or they may be present only to our thought. In either case they elicit from us a reaction...."

At a transformative moment, a constellation of tradition, relationships, meanings, hopes, and fears is present in the worshiping community. There is the covenant that each individual has committed to honor and engage as a member of the community. There also has to be something that none of the practices, preparations, and participation in covenantal community can create—and that is a moment of grace.

In Unitarian Universalist religious life, grace gets too little credit, because the word is used by religious traditions that make many of us uncomfortable. For us, grace simply means a gift that we did not create, could not earn, and cannot control. People want to give the minister credit when they experience it. Ministers wish they knew all the ways that it happens, and how to invite grace in more skillfully. Worship leaders invite and respond to such moments, however, not through control but through gratitude. When lives are changed through worship, it happens because we all do it together, in ways we will never fully understand.

FOUR TRANSFORMATIVE
WORSHIP SERVICES

When we finished our sabbatical travels, we considered which services remained with us most powerfully and eventually settled on four of them. We present them here based on descriptions we wrote as web logs soon after leaving the services. Although these services represented different religious traditions, sizes of congregation, and geographical locations, they shared several qualities that made them feel special to us. Considered together, these qualities may point to a future direction for creativity and innovation in Unitarian Universalist worship practices.

- "Retraditioning" worship practices for a new generation.

- Creative adaptation of the worship space available for the service.

- Musical involvement, regardless of the style of music used.

- Engagement of all the senses.

- Attention to every detail producing a smoothly flowing liturgy.

- Inclusivity, whether you were parishioner or guest, young or old, believer or non-believer.

Retraditioning. While evident in the Catholic and Episcopal services we attended, the idea of retraditioning is well established in Unitarian Universalist worship practice. We have long adapted traditional elements of worship through changes in wording or symbolism. The sanctuary of All Souls Church in Washington, D.C. can lead the first-time visitor to expect congregational Protestant formality and tradition, but the entry into holy time through the bells, chalice, and celebrative processional quickly change the expectations in the direction of inclusive celebration. Liturgical devices common in United Methodist worship were retraditioned at the 11:11 Fort Worth service by the use of an electric country band to accompany the hymns, the choice of an Irish blessing for the choral benediction, and the interaction between the lectionary reading and the homily.

Creative Use of Worship Spaces. Three of the four services had no more than two hundred people attending, allowing innovative seating arrangements and movement to different locations for certain parts of the service. All Souls was the most traditional sanctuary and the largest congregation of the four. However, even there, a dancer's use of the chancel space, the relationship of the choir to the congregation, and the intimacy of the preaching experience all suggested creative possibilities for making the best use of the space.

Musical Involvement. These services used traditional hymns, new praise songs, chants, plainsong, country pop songs, classical music, and organ pieces. What all these services had in common was that there was no sense of separation from the music. Even the pieces that were performed invited participation through the way they engaged the themes and connected the service elements.

Engagement of All Senses. The Catholics used incense and bells; the Episcopalians used colorful art on the walls and in their vestments; the United Methodists used an incense ceremony and video; and the Unitarian Universalists used song leadership, dance, and visuals for a children's story. In each service, there was multisensory experience that invited an opening of the heart as well as the mind.

Attention to Detail. The overall experience was close to seamless in each service. Service participants were well rehearsed or inherently skillful in their roles, and the transitions from one part of the service to the next were smooth. The congregation was able to totally engage with what was being presented and remain unaware of how it happened.

Inclusivity. Although three of the services were from other traditions and the UU service was at a church unfamiliar to us, we never felt like outsiders. For the highly liturgical Catholic and Episcopal services, the personal or written instruction we received made us feel comfortable and involved. The formality of these service structures created a vessel that could hold a certain amount of informality, in the form of instruction or humor, that made us feel at ease. We did not feel that we had to believe in the theological assumptions of each service to be touched by its spirit.

Regardless of the size of your congregation or the character of your worship space, and whether you are exploring transformative worship in your regular service or considering a second service with a different style, we believe that incorporating these six qualities will make a tremendous difference in your congregation's worship life. Transformative worship does not come about as a result of one Sunday's service, one new element of worship, or one quality of worship life introduced and sustained. It comes about because there is attention paid to many elements all at once, Sunday after Sunday, so that the transformed lives of the members reflect back in their participation and appreciation of all that the service offers.

St. Peter's Roman Catholic Church
Cleveland, Ohio

We attended two services, Palm Sunday and the Easter Vigil, at Saint Peter's in Cleveland (formally named Historic Saint Peter Church), a congregation which is known for its liturgical innovativeness. The first thing we noticed at the Easter vigil was how the worship space was arranged in three stations: the main area with chairs placed in two semicircles so that members of the congregation faced one another; a large communion table on a raised stage area; and a baptismal font. Throughout the service, which included a baptism, all three areas were used.

The Catholic Church is known for its high liturgy, and St. Peter's was no exception. Incense was heavily used, as were bells to mark the beginning or ending of certain parts of the liturgy. The order of service was minimal, listing the barest essentials of the worship service. In many respects the liturgy was standard for a Catholic mass.

Processional with Children. The service began with a children's processional in which all children participated. Bell ringers processed in first, looking dignified and focused on their task. Children remained with their parents for the entire service, and by and large, they were respectful and worshipful along with their parents.

Passion Story. On Palm Sunday, the mass had some unique elements. Instead of a homily, the Passion Story was read in entirety by three alternating lay readers. The readers were obviously trained or rehearsed, as they were clearly audible and easy to listen to. We stood for the entire reading of the Gospel. There was plenty of space for prayer, silence, and listening to the music. Nothing seemed rushed.

144

The Gospel text was interspersed with a simple, two- or three-line responsive song that was repeated throughout the reading. Although it could have been boring, we found it comforting to keep coming back to that one piece of music, singing it and feeling it differently each time.

Communion. The entire congregation was invited to get up from their chairs and surround the communion table. There was no suggestion that anyone who was not Catholic should stay back. The priest chanted and intoned prayers, which the congregation responded to by heart. Somehow, the entire congregation was fed and drank from one piece of flatbread and one bottle of wine. We couldn't help but think of the loaves and fishes.

Hymns. The choir was small, no more than twenty people. Sounding like one voice, they sang *Hosanna Filio David, Domine Deus* (C. Penfield) and *O Domine Jesu Christe* (G. Palestrina). An extremely skilled pianist and an oboist added even more beauty. The music was spare in a way, not bold or bombastic, but it complemented the somber mood of the service, and we were completely taken aback by its simple beauty. At the end of the Gospel reading, the pianist began to play just underneath the readings, so as not to distract from them but to enhance the feeling of drama. It was otherworldly and very much of this world—all at the same time.

Although there were many aspects of this particular worship experience that made it transformative, we were particularly aware of the attention paid to every detail, from the moment we walked into the door to the social hour after the service. Readers of the Gospel were chosen with obvious care; they approached their role as liturgists with serious intention. The homily at the Easter Service was thoughtful, well crafted, and relevant. It was noticeably easy for a newcomer who had never experienced Catholic liturgy to participate. And finally, the sense that, no matter what their place in life, all were welcome was both a relief and a joy. Afterwards, several members of St. Peter's were sprinkled throughout the congregation, talking to newcomers. A welcome table was visible, but not overwhelming. We felt as if we had been invited to a luxurious home where no expense had been spared to put us at ease.

At St. Peter's there was not one individual transformative moment. Instead, the entire experience—from physically moving about the space to multisensory engagement to the attention to detail—conspired to leave worshipers in a different place than when they entered. It was a truly memorable ninety minutes, which felt both completely in the moment and utterly and ultimately timeless.

WHAT WE LEARNED

- The physical placement of chairs made a large, somewhat empty space feel welcoming.

- Reaching out to visitors can make a big difference. The man who said to us, "You'll be back" made us feel like part of the congregation.

- Being able to see people's faces in worship and communion encourages a feeling of being part of the service.

- Excellent music can really heighten the worship experience. The choir sounded like one voice and was inspiring. The simple sound of the oboe transported us.

- Appealing to the senses, such as using incense, adds another dimension to the worship experience.

- Having children in worship can be wonderful. The children were respectful, and we sensed that they somehow knew it was holy time.

- Short, simple, repetitive songs help worshipers to experience the liturgy more deeply.

- Excellent preparation makes for a seamless worship experience.

- An absolutely spotless and well-maintained building provides an inspiring setting for worship.

SAINT GREGORY OF NYSSA
SAN FRANCISCO, CALIFORNIA

We were particularly excited about attending Saint Gregory of Nyssa Episcopal Church, located in a working- to middle-class San Francisco neighborhood called Portrero Hill. We had found their website after reading about them in *Christian Century* over a year earlier, and we were deeply interested in hearing more about their innovative worship services. We had also read about their icon project; they had commissioned an artist to decorate their walls with murals featuring a wide variety of historic and contemporary figures—from St. Paul to Malcolm X—holding hands and dancing.

The liturgy was a wonderful example of the practice of retraditioning in the Episcopal Church. Rather than relying on the megachurch approach of the 1980s and 1990s, this church has revived early Christian practices that included dance and movement. St. Gregory's had been honing and perfecting its liturgy for almost thirty years. They had functioned in relative obscurity until the *New York Times* published an article about their worship in 1996. After that, they received attention in many religious media, and they published a book of the songs and chants they use for their liturgy, as well as a video. Please note that the congregation's own extremely detailed descriptions and resources describing the evolution and theory liturgy at St. Gregory's are readily available on their website (www. saintgregorys.org). Richard Fabian is the founding rector and works in a team with Donald Schell. They say on their website:

In 1978 the Bishop and Convention of the Episcopal Dio-
cese of California organized the Church of St. Gregory
Nyssa at San Francisco, honoring a fourth-century Greek
theologian whose teaching has enriched eastern and western churches alike. Our charter charged us to continue
liturgical development in the direction the new Book of
Common Prayer had set out. We were to draw directly on
the classical resources that inspired this prayer book—
including Jewish and eastern Christian resources, newly
emphasized in this version—for practices which would
enhance congregational participation. And we were to
build congregational music, dance, and other expressions
beyond what settled parishes might readily attempt. Our
goal was not a unique "experimental" or "eastern" liturgy,
but a liturgy embodying an authentic Anglican approach,
gaining from modern scholarship, open to new material,
and yielding experience to serve the whole Church.

As we approached the church on the second Sunday in Advent,
2005, we saw a relatively new building suitable for a small to midsized congregation. A man standing outside the front door welcomed
us and handed us each a thick liturgy booklet. Although we were a
little anxious because we thought we were late, he assured us that
the singing that was going on in the sanctuary was actually practice:
The congregation was practicing the hymns that would be sung that
morning. He was very personable and helpful, and when he found out
we were UU clergy he told us about his friendship with a colleague of
ours.

There were no orders of service given to us. As we came in, we were
greeted with smiles and eye contact. We made nametags for ourselves,
using red markers because we were first-time visitors; repeat visitors
used black. This distinction was helpful for the church members, who
had buttons that served as nametags. They then could help us out by
name with certain parts of the liturgy where names were spoken. We
joined the crowd who had gathered around the communion altar in

the center of the room. The congregation seemed to be virtually all white baby boomers and Gen-Xers.

Words can hardly describe the unique space that is St. Gregory's. It was designed and built about fifteen years into the life of the congregation expressly to complement their style of worship. The first thing we saw when we entered was the communion table in the center of the room. The placement of the table is intentional—that is, that communion is available and open to all; there are no barriers. On the far side of the space were glass doors that opened to a huge rock fountain sculpture used for baptisms. When we looked up, we were surrounded by dancing saints. It is difficult to capture the beauty, ingenuity, and creativity of the artwork in words.

The seated portion of the service took place in an adjacent sanctuary. There were no fixed pews, no center pulpit, not even a fixed altar area. Two hundred seats were arranged on three sides of the chancel. Although the worship leader wore beautifully colored vestments and the priest delivered the sermon from a slightly elevated chair, there was a clear effort to convey a non-hierarchical sense. The room was also filled with wonderful liturgical objects from different parts of the world that were used in or decorated the service. Most notably, fringed parasols from India added to the color of the processional. There was no written order of service, but full scripts of their order of service are available on their website.

Hymn Practice. Joining a circle around the communion table, we began by practicing the hymns to be sung during the service. Their liturgy book was an amazing resource of eclectic tunes, ranging from third-century Byzantine hymns to Bobby McFerrin's version of the Twenty-third Psalm. We were then instructed to move from the practice/communion area to the sanctuary, which we did as a group.

Hymn Singing. The music director kept the music moving along at a lively tempo; we were not allowed to pause at the end of each phrase. This kept the energy flowing, but it sometimes was difficult to keep up with the pace. The congregation's beautiful singing encouraged people to join in, even on complex hymns that were difficult for some to sing on tune. We had been told as we entered that the members of the choir did not sit in a special group during the liturgy but were scattered among the people in the sanctuary. The choir's anthems were sung later during the communion around the table.

Silence. We entered into silence with a series of seven or eight bell sounds, and then we sat together for about two minutes in complete and total silence. We loved sitting this way, smelling the incense, and then coming out of the silence with more bell sounds.

Liturgy of the Word. The prayers were done in a beautifully inclusive way. The leaders read a script inviting people to offer their prayers from the congregation. Several liturgy leaders had scripted texts that were a regular part of this section, and a sequence in which they were offered. These texts were interwoven with the brief prayers offered from the congregation. The congregation sang versicles such as "Lord, hear our prayer" after each speaker.

Psalm and Gospel Reading. Lay members of the congregation read or sang the Gospel standing in a designated area among the congregation.

Homily. A newly ordained priest gave a ten-minute homily in which he talked about the importance of the Christian faith as telling a story and making a dialogue possible. He also expressed his gratitude to the congregation for its participation in his own faith journey. The script for the liturgy instructs the preacher to always include an interpretive commentary on one or more of the readings, and a narrative from the preacher's own experience.

Sermon Response. This time was prefaced by the priest, who said that "the Holy Spirit may be speaking to us all—perhaps some of you right now—and she also speaks to us in silence." His words were an invitation for people to stand up and share what was on their minds and hearts. About three or four people offered thoughtful and heartfelt insights, and no one misused the time or spoke too long. In UU congregations, this time might be called a talkback, offering the opportunity for people to reflect on or challenge the sermon, but the quality of interaction was much more deeply reflective than most UU talkbacks we have experienced.

Gospel Procession. We were instructed to either touch the Bible as it processed through the congregation, or touch the shoulder of someone who had touched the Bible. This reminded us of how, regardless of any love/hate relationship with the Bible, it is like an old relative that still commands respect and affection. In the Jewish Shabbat service, the Torah is paraded through the congregation and we've always admired that ritual. This practice was similar.

Announcements. These were delivered by a lay leader, from the center of the congregation. They were concise and well done. People were invited afterwards to stay for coffee and refreshments, get a tour of the building, receive a blessing from the new priest, or come to the chancel for healing prayers. Children were brought into the service at this point to be included in the Eucharist.

Eucharist. After the announcements, we were asked to move from our chairs to the space around the communion table. We were to touch the shoulder of the person in front of us and move in a certain way—step right leg forward, step left leg forward, step back. Then we surrounded the communion table and the process of taking communion was explained.

It was stressed from the very beginning that the communion table was open to all. The new priest offered the story of the first communion in the traditional words, and the liturgy leaders first offered communion to each other, addressing one another by name, and then to the people. It seemed like many choir members were served first, because the choir was then able to gather at one end of the communion table and sing as the ritual continued. The meaning behind this style of communion is that there is no rail or altar or barrier to communion, but that people in community feed one another, calling one another by name as they do so (e.g., "The Body of Christ, broken for you, Kathleen").

The Eucharist is a powerful ritual. At St. Gregory's, it was personal and individual as well as a community event. However, it felt chaotic and rushed at times. The bread was broken, and the cup passed around the circle, very quickly. Furthermore, as first-time visitors, we found that the distinction between wine and grape juice was not clear.

There were no provisions for simply dipping the bread into the wine, a practice known as intinction.

Invitation to the Dance. We were taught a simple dance that asked us to cross right leg front, left leg back, right leg front, then raise our left and right knee. In general, we liked the innovation of being involved in worship with not only our minds, but also our bodies. It was fun to circle around the altar. This section demonstrated that worship is not a performance-oriented event; it is participatory. No other worship service we attended strove to embody this concept more than Saint Gregory's.

Singing Celebration of Birthdays and Anniversaries. This was a ritual unique to Saint Gregory's that both of us loved. Before the service closed, members with birthdays or anniversaries that week were brought forward. The rector prayed for them by name and the congregation responded with a song: "Lord, give them many years."

WHAT WE LEARNED

- Using different colors for nametags is a simple technique for distinguishing first-time visitors from repeat visitors.

- Creative aesthetic accoutrements to worship, such as the fringed umbrellas, bells, and incense, engage different senses and create a feeling that one has moved into holy time.

- Instructions about what comes next in the service helps the service move along briskly and enables lay leaders to play their parts flawlessly. However, at times this can feel too much like script reading.

- Bell introductions and well-timed silences can punctuate the service and create a sense of transition from one element to another.

- There are creative possibilities for engaging the body in honoring holy symbols, even within the UU tradition.

- A personable and liturgically articulate congregation is very engaging to a first-time visitor. No one we spoke with asked us for our opinion about the service, but they were completely at home answering any questions about it.

- Although orders of service can be cumbersome to hold and feel "in-house," they help make visitors feel more at ease with what is going to happen in the service and what is expected of them.

- Stressing that everyone is welcome at the communion table means that attention must be paid to those who can't partake of communion if alternatives to wine and wheat are not served. Visitors who are physically handicapped also need to be considered.

- Even in a small worship space, not having speakers use a microphone is a barrier for those who are hard of hearing or who simply can't hear because of where they are sitting. If speakers are not using microphones, they must project their voices.

- Birthdays and anniversaries can be creatively honored in worship in a liturgically coherent manner.

First United Methodist
Fort Worth, Texas

———————◆●◆———————

At First United Methodist Church, Fort Worth, Texas, we attended a contemporary worship service that was not based on the evangelical praise service model, but instead on ideas drawn from Matthew Fox's creation spirituality teachings, and music from contemporary country, folk, and pop sources. It was called the 11:11 service because it began at 11:11 AM. It ran at the same time as the second of the church's traditional services in the sanctuary, which began at 11:00, and it was called roundtable worship, because it took place in a circle around a common table.

We arrived early enough to explore their attractive sanctuary, which seats about seven hundred, and to review their traditional service liturgy. Both of us appreciate many things about traditional liturgy, and we could quickly see that this was a church that paid careful attention to its worship life. The congregation members leaving the first service were dominated by "civic generation" elders born before 1945 and baby boomers, some with their kids. Younger families were not as much in evidence.

Before and after the 11:11 service, we had a chance to chat with paid staff and volunteers who had contributed to making this service happen. The associate pastor, Linda McDermott, told us that the service was initially started for all the usual reasons associated with growth goals and attracting younger members. However, they found that the mix of people who came were not just interested in a different kind of music or liturgy; they wanted to engage in church in a different way, so the leaders of the service were trying to add other educational and social opportunities. Her observations brought to mind a book we were reading at the time of this visit: *The Practicing Church* by Diana Butler Bass. Bass describes how vital mainline Protestant churches are thriving by attracting people who are serious about their spiritual lives, who are open to both old and new forms of worship and spiritual practice, and who see their church involvement as a gate to a way of life, rather than just a membership in another civic organization.

Besides the leader of the band, who was married to the associate pastor and was ordained clergy himself, the service was supported each week by at least two volunteers who managed the sound board and PowerPoint presentations. The social hall where the service was held had been renovated with state-of-the-art back-projection screens at both ends, a wonderful sound system, and stage-quality track lighting. The liturgy and song words were projected on the screens and available in a large-sized order of service. Charles Gaby, who developed the service along with fellow clergy Linda McDermott and Jim Connor, told us that they tried to follow Matthew Fox's "Creation Spirituality" path throughout the liturgical calendar year, as well as within each service. The path consists of:

- *Via Positiva* (summer; themes of in-gathering and celebration)

- *Via Negativa* (fall; themes of contemplation, silence, making room for the mystery)

- *Festival Times* (from Thanksgiving to Christmas)

- *Via Creativa* (winter; themes of bringing something to birth in the midst of winter)

- *Via Transformativa* (spring; themes of Easter, resurrection, the transformative power of life, sending forth, transformation by the word)

The service we attended was the last in a series of services on the Via Negativa. The series title was "Whistling in the Dark." It had five sections, outlined in the order of service. A series of meditations on the theme of the day, consisting of quotes from spiritual writers mostly from outside the Christian tradition was also printed in the order of service.

Gathering and Opening. The Gathering and Opening acts comprised the Via Positiva section of the service. Charles had previously told us: "We don't try to set a mood—we don't tell people to be quiet—we just let them be. The band does the prelude. Our purpose is not to talk about God, but to invoke God's presence." We found it a little annoying that people near us continued to chat during the prelude, even though others nearby were clearly interested in settling in with the music.

The Gathering act consisted of the arriving formalities, the prelude, and the welcome by the bandleader. The welcome transitioned into the opening, which began with "Wake Up," an original song. We all stood and sang it together. One sample verse is: "The past is a memory, the next thing is a mystery, from different roads we came, yet somehow it's all the same – Wake up, wake up – the dawn is near!" This song would work well in a UU contemporary service, although with no preservice singing of new songs, we found ourselves stumbling over some unfamiliar rhythms. Since they used the screens to project the words, and also had an order of service, it would have been helpful to include the music in at least one of these media.

Following the song, Charles came out from behind the piano and did the Invocation as a short, spontaneous prayer accompanied by the lighting of copal—a kind of resin that offers a light smell similar to incense or sage. We enjoyed the engagement of our sense of smell as we created the sacred space. Then he invited us to greet one another with wishes of peace. From visiting other churches, we've learned that we prefer to ritualize this with formal words, such as "Peace be with you," along with introductions by name, but that was not suggested.

Learning. This act, the Via Negativa section, was for the reading of the scriptures, which were usually drawn from the biblical lectionary readings for that Sunday. The psalm for the day was read in unison and was not connected to the day's sermon or theme. It was Psalm

100, "Make a Joyful Noise Unto the Lord," the sort of psalm that can go with almost any worship service except a funeral.

The second scripture reading was the parable of the talents from Matthew 25, and we were intrigued by how this reading would be connected to the sermon, which was titled "What We Resist, Persists."

Accepting. Although Charles described the first part of this act, the time for praying, as part of Via Negativa, and the last part, the sermon, as part of Via Creativa, none of this was made explicit in the order of service. He explained that in the prayer time they led people into the silence with a doxology-like verse, often drawn from folk or contemporary country sources, such as these lines from Robert Hunter's "Ripple," a Grateful Dead classic. The words are:

> Reach out your hand, if your cup be empty,
> If your cup is full, may it be again.
> Let it be known, there is a fountain
> That was not made by the hands of men.

We sang the verse three times, there was some silent time accompanied by a beautiful Native American flute, and then a lay leader came forward to lead the spoken prayer.

Charles had told us that after prayer time they sometimes used a video clip or drama, but that was not part of the service we attended. Instead there was a performance piece by the band, a lovely song called "Dust," by Erika Luckett.

The sermon followed, a twenty-five minute reflection that was more psychological than theological in its spiritual advice regarding letting go of wounds and grudges. We appreciated the sermon and recognized that his preaching style on this particular Sunday (which would have fit well in a UU setting) was complemented by the styles of other clergy and lay leaders on staff who offered occasional sermons.

Blessing. This fifth act was the final part of the Via Creativa section. After the sermon, the offering was invited. The congregation brought their gifts to the table at the center of the chair circles, which served as the altar. We got up from our seats and with 170 of us in the room it took a little time to do this, but it felt good.

The band was singing an offertory song as we came forward and returned to our seats. We had been told they usually used the same song for a season and then changed it. For this season, mid-November, the song was "Now Thank We All Our God," a traditional Thanksgiving hymn, done with a great lively rhythm by the country-rock style band. We loved singing it with them as we waited for others to make their offerings.

The last part of the blessing section was not specifically outlined in the order of service, but Charles had previously told us it was the Via Transformativa part of the service. Prior to the closing prayer, the band played what was described to us as the service's regular closing song: "May the Road Rise to Meet You." After playing the song one time through, the band continued the tune behind Charles as he made some quick announcements related to the church community and then invited people to ask for prayers and blessings in a public way.

Following these spoken prayers and blessings, the band struck up the verses to "May the Road Rise to Meet You" again, and the service ended. No postlude was played.

WHAT WE LEARNED

- A creative contemporary service doesn't have to use evangelical praise music and can fit very well in a UU setting.

- People who attend the contemporary service at this church come to be part of a community of spiritual practice, rather than to be members of a civic institution where they have friends.

- It takes a crew of at least three to four paid or volunteer staff plus the band to manage a contemporary service on a weekly basis.

- There is plenty of softer contemporary music with religious themes that can be used to create contemporary worship without rock and roll praise music. You don't even have to use the whole song; single suitable verses can be used in doxology style.

- The model of worship that is suggested by Matthew Fox's creation spirituality has lots of potential for informing contemporary worship services that would work well in any UU context.

All Souls Church, Unitarian
Washington, D.C.

———————◆●◆———————

All Souls Church, Unitarian was a "must" stop on our list. Several members of West Shore had visited All Souls and were deeply impressed with their liturgy and worship. Their minister, Rev. Rob Hardies, has led a revival of excitement and strength in the life of the church since 2001, working closely with Director of Music John Strang.

All Souls is the Washington area's "mother" church, dating from the mid-twentieth-century ministry of A. Powell Davies, who inspired no fewer than eight start-up churches around the Washington area. The church sits at 16th NW and Harvard, the intersection of several multicultural neighborhoods in DC. The building is modeled after St. Martin's in the Fields in London, and seats at least five hundred between the main floor and wraparound balcony. It has a large and excellent organ and a high central pulpit. Many aspects of the worship and the music program existed before either Hardies or Strang joined the staff. There have long been two adult choirs, the All Souls Choir and the Jubilee Singers. Although both choirs reflect the multiracial make-up of the congregation, Jubilee Singers has been devoted to exploring gospel, African-American, and world choral music. Strang has also started a Children's Choir. The congregation also has a long tradition of fine organ music and great preaching.

On the Sunday we attended, the church was full to the rafters since it was the weekend of an antiwar demonstration and many UUs from out of town were present. Here are some of the more striking elements of an All Souls service:

Lighting of the Chalice. The chalice lighting called us to silence in preparation for the music for meditation. The effect was twofold: It calmed the chaos of what was happening outside the sanctuary so that people could prepare themselves to be in a space for worship, and it led nicely into the music for meditation. In the order of service, this instruction is given: "During the Music for Meditation, all are invited to come forward to light a candle of joy or concern from the chalice flame. At the sounding of the chime, the congregation rises."

Music from Artists in Residence. Because of his commitment to musical diversity, John has hired musicians with particular expertise and made them artists in residence, with a commitment to perform a certain number of Sundays during the year. This is one of the most exciting aspects of All Souls's music program. For example, just on the one Sunday we attended, a jazz artist and a percussionist enhanced the service with music for the meditation part of the service. John has built a relationship with such people over the years, and they feel part of the liturgical life of All Souls. The choir uses some paid section leaders who are understood as artists in residence as well. They have a clear idea of when they will be singing and are used for particular musical styles, depending on their talents and interests. Their involvement improves the quality and consistency of the singing.

Processional Hymn. Each week, the choir, liturgists, service participants, minister, and others begin the service with a processional down the center aisle to a processional hymn. There is a stable of regular hymns that the congregation knows by heart, which allows members to "own" the processional. Often the procession is accompanied by African drums or another kind of percussion instrument. The choir usually remains on the main floor. Over the last four years, they have moved away from doing a majority of their choral contributions from the choir loft. The choir also contributes at least three pieces to the service.

Concerns for Our World and Prayers. On the Sunday we attended, this section was done by Rev. William Sinkford, president of the UUA. It was beautifully and thoughtfully done as a prayer inclusive of both global concerns and naming individuals in the congregation.

Call to Meditation. The call to meditation was a musical piece, followed by silence that was underscored by gentle wind chimes. The end of the meditation was the singing of "Spirit of Life," which the congregation does every week and knows by heart. We both loved the wind chimes, which the organist/music director sounded from the choir loft.

Reading. Rob chose an excerpt from Lao Tzu's *Tao Te Ching* that fit the theme of the day beautifully.

Sermon. "Violence and Redemption" was the title of Rob's sermon that Sunday. It was well crafted, beautifully delivered, and appropriate for the day, which included dozens of visitors who attended the march on Washington that weekend.

Offering of Gifts and Music. This was a particularly powerful and effective piece of the worship experience. Rob told the story of how after the United States dropped the bomb on Hiroshima, the children of All Souls sent school supplies to the children of Hiroshima, and the children of Hiroshima sent artwork back. Projected on the wall behind the pulpit were pictures of the children's artwork. An amazing piece of organ music by a contemporary Japanese composer, Takashi Sakai, accompanied the PowerPoint presentation. Then, Ken Yamaguchi-Clark, their dancer-in-residence, offered a dance in response to the pictures and music. He moved gracefully around the limited space in front of the pulpit, and actually climbed and balanced on the banister of the pulpit stairway. We were reminded that it is possible to have effective liturgical dance with only one dancer and a fairly limited space. This was a beautiful and amazing combination of three types of art—visual, music and dance.

Usually worship associates announce the offering. They typically speak in their own words about why they give to the church.

Benediction in Music. As the All Souls choir performed "Lay Aside Weight," by Glenn Burleigh, the entire church wound up on their feet, clapping and swaying and moving with the music. Although the content of the service was very heavy, the ending was joyful. A pianist, a percussionist, and about thirty singers stood closely together up front. They were lively and animated, and sang perfectly, with a trained vocalist riffing on top of the melody line. The liturgists and ministers stayed up front for this celebrative piece, and stood and danced and sang with the choir.

It was fantastic to be in a UU church that was packed to the rafters. We had to pull out folding chairs to get a spot in the balcony. The whole experience felt very fresh and alive, yet deep. The liturgy was orchestrated in a way that moved the participants from states of passivity to activity; from focused to unfocused and back to focused intellectual and emotional stimulation; from joyous celebration to quietude—in short, from the heights to the depths and back home again. We left feeling we had truly experienced a transformative UU worship.

WHAT WE LEARNED

- Artists in residence can become a regular part of the worship life of the church and improve the quality and consistency of the congregation's singing.

- High-quality worship can help a church grow. Rob told us that the church invested greater financial resources in the music program than they had been accustomed to doing during the first two years of his ministry, hoping this risk would be rewarded by membership and pledge growth in future years; so far that risk has paid off. Good worship must be accompanied by good small group programming and other vehicles for involvement; but worship is the gateway.

- The role of liturgical "producer" is an important staff position for larger congregations to consider. We saw this role up close in two different congregations, Cedar Ridge and All Souls, Unitarian. At Cedar Ridge, the role was filled by a full-time lay staff member who managed a technologically sophisticated service involving contributions from up to four different worship teams. At All Souls, with less technological sophistication and a liturgy that followed a similar pattern every week, the transitions from spoken to musical and artistic pieces in the service primarily fell to the music director to manage. Rob and John told us that they don't necessarily have to meet every week in person to be able to make the components and transitions of the service work together smoothly.

- Using multiple choral leaders allows congregations to use different choral styles equally well in worship. The Jubilee Singers at All Souls work with their own choral director. John realizes that multiple choral styles enhance the service and that he can't lead all of them equally well.

- Using a stable of processional hymns that the congregation will ultimately know by heart (even though they are always printed in the order of service) starts the service strongly, in a celebrative and participatory mode.

- We were intrigued to realize that you can have musical diversity without a house band. Although All Souls owns a drum set and has a percussionist in residence whom they use every month, and although services may feature songs with electric bass or guitar, they do not recruit volunteers for or pay a house band. The musical diversity arises from the choral selections, the many percussion instruments, the way the organ is used to play other than conventional organ pieces, the use of diverse instrumentation, and the presence of guest artists.

- Heritage and theology matter as much as diversity. We often have said to people who talk to us about visiting All Souls that the racial diversity of the congregation is an important reason why they have been able to sustain a rich liturgical and musical life. While that is true, African American members comprise only about 20 percent of the congregation. Rob and John attribute the commitment to excellence and diversity in worship to the church's long-term identity as a place where excellence in music and liturgy matters, and to a comfort the church has always had with its Christian roots and with theistic language, despite having been served by ministers with humanist identities. The church's humanist heritage is joyful and celebrative, and they feel comfortable with using all the arts that arise from the heritage of Christian worship that they share.

RESOURCES

Some of the books and essays below are available only online or through libraries. Many are available through the publishers or through the UUA Bookstore, which regularly stocks resources for use in worship: www.uua.org/bookstore; 800-215-9076.

Alexander, Scott. *The Relational Pulpit: Closing the Gap Between Preacher and Pew*. Boston: Skinner House Books, 1993. A widely read text on UU preaching.

Bass, Diana, and Joseph Stewart-Sicking. *From Nomads to Pilgrims: Stories from Practicing Congregations*. Herndon, VA: Alban Institute, 2005. Vital Christian mainline congregations tell their stories.

Bass, Diana. *The Practicing Congregation: Imagining a New Old Church*. Herndon, VA: Alban Institute, 2004. An influential vision for mainline congregational renewal through "re-traditioning" worship and spiritual practices.

Brandenburg, Ellen, ed. *The Seven Principles in Word and Worship*. Boston: Skinner House Books, 2007. Resources for liturgical affirmation of the seven UU Principles.

Congregation of Abraxas. "Worship Reader." Newport, RI: Congregation of Abraxas, 1980. Various essays and service texts from a small but influential order of Unitarian Universalists concerned with worship as spiritual practice, active from 1975 to 1985. Available in certain libraries and at several online web addresses.

Kimball, Dan. *Emerging Worship: Creating Worship Gatherings for New Generations.* Grand Rapids, MI: Zondervan, 2004. Widely read manual for the new worship styles in the evangelical "emergent church" movement.

Long, Thomas. *Beyond the Worship Wars: Building Vital and Faithful Worship.* Herndon, VA: Alban Institute, 2001. Insightful contemporary reflections from an Emory professor on the tensions in worship preferences in Protestant congregations.

McFee, Marsha. *The Worship Workshop: Creative Ways to Design Worship Together.* Nashville: Abingdon, 2002. Ideas from a dynamic creative worship consultant. Also of interest is McFee's presentation to the 2007 UUA Conference on Contemporary Worship, recorded on the DVD "Ideas for Worship."

Merkert, Angela, and Ken Brown. Resources for conceptualizing changes in worship styles and an excellent bibliography on "Emergent Forms for Liberal Worship" from two UU congregational consultants. www.merkertbrown.com.

Pagitt, Doug. *Reimagining Spiritual Formation: A Week in the Life of an Experimental Church.* Grand Rapids, MI: Zondervan, 2004. Blogs and reflections from the early years of an influential emergent Christian church in Minneapolis.

Pickett, Helen. *Rejoice Together: Prayers, Meditations and Other Readings for Family, Individual and Small-Group Worship,* Second Edition. Boston: Skinner House Books, 2005. A widely used UU worship resource book.

Rzepka, Jane, and Ken Sawyer. *Thematic Preaching: An Introduction.* St. Louis: Chalice Press, 2001. Influential book on preaching widely read by UU ministers.

Schulman, Frank. *A Manual of Worship*. Boston: Unitarian Universalist Association, 2006. Although recently published, Schulman's manual reflects a classic early twentieth-century worship aesthetic.

Schulz, William, ed. *Transforming Words: Six Essays on Preaching*. Boston: Skinner House Books, 1996. Sparkling essays on preaching, including Roy Phillips's reflections on "sermon as sacrament".

Skinner, Clarence. *Religion and the Well Ordered Life*. Boston: Universalist Historical Society, 1955. Classic Universalist reflection on the spiritual practice of a liberal religious life.

———. "Worship and a Well Ordered Life." In *The Essential Clarence Skinner* by Charles Howe. Boston: Skinner House Books, 2005. Excerpt specifically about worship from *Religion and the Well Ordered Life*, noted above, included in this recent collection.

Unitarian Universalist Association. Resources include "Leading Congregations in Worship" by the Commission on Common Worship (1985); "Considerations for Cultural Borrowing: Questions to Ask (and Answer)" by the 2003 UUA Cultural (Mis)Appropriations Ad Hoc Committee; and the Worship Web, which contains a searchable database of worship materials. www.uua.org.

Vogt, Von Ogden. *Art and Religion*. New Haven, CT: Yale University Press, 1921. Early twentieth century classic Unitarian reflection on the worship arts.

———. *The Primacy of Worship*. Boston: Starr King Press, 1958. The manifesto of the greatest Unitarian liturgist of the early twentieth century.

ACKNOWLEDGMENTS

We thank the many friends and colleagues who hosted us on our 2005-2006 sabbatical and/or gave generously of their time and wisdom in interviews. Many took time away from their day at short notice to talk at length with us about worship. This book could not have happened without those enriching conversations. We thank: Doug Wilson; John Gibbons and Sue Baldauf; Mark Belletini; Earl Holt; John Buehrens; Barbara and Jaco Ten Hove; Rob Hardies; John Strang; Ken Belden; Tom Schade; Thomas Anastazi; Ron Robinson; Marlin Lavanhar; Felicia Urbanski; Jim Brown; Jason Shelton; Burton Carley; Rob and Janne Eller-Isaacs; Kendyl Gibbons; Ryan Torma; Doug Padgitt; Bill Burke; Anthony David; Christine Tata; James and Nan Hobart; Mark and Becky Edmiston-Lange; Charles Gaby; Len Deloney; Laurel Hallman; Dennis Hamilton; Craig Roshaven; David Keyes; Betsy Mitchell-Heaning; Art Lavoie; Robin Stover and her mother, Irene; Mary Grinnell and Lisa Colvin; Kelly Ratliff and Dan Chaffin; Michael Tino; Arvid Straube; Ken Brown; Angela Merkert; and Roshi John Daido Loori.

We particularly acknowledge and express gratitude for the contributions of Kathy Strawser and Tamara Lebak. Their original ideas and leadership in developing the mode of intergenerational worship at West Shore Church are reflected in the sections on that topic. Beyond that, in their roles as Lifespan Faith Development Director and Sabbatical Minister respectively, Kathy and Tamara helped make the book possible and were our creative collaborators in worship preparation during the years this book took form.

169

The sixteen members of the Winter 2006 Worship Associates Class at West Shore Church offered thoughtful engagement with the ideas in this book and helped to shape its contents.

Our editors at Skinner House, Mary Benard and Marshall Hawkins, have been encouraging, supportive, and critical in just the right ways. We are very grateful to them.

Finally, Wayne would like to remember and thank his old friends from the Congregation of Abraxas, who instilled in him a passion for and fascination with worship as spiritual practice: Vern Barnet, Fred Gillis, Duke Gray, Harry Thor, Stephan Papa, Mark Belletini, Richard Boeke, Kitsy Winthrop, and David McMillan.